by Gerard Malanga

POETRY

3 Poems for Benedetta Barzini (1967)
Prelude to International Velvet Debutante (1967)
The Last Benedetta Poems (1969)
Gerard Malanga Selbsportrat eines Dichters (1970)
10 Poems for 10 Poets (1970)
chic death (1971)
Wheels of Light (1972)
The Poetry of Night, Dawn and Dream/Nine Poems for Cesar Vallejo (1972)
Licht/Light (1973, bilingual)
Incarnations: Poems 1965–1971 (1974)
Rosebud (1975)
Leaping Over Gravestones (1976)
Ten Years After: The Selected Benedetta Poems (1977)
100 years have passed (1978)
This Will Kill That (1983)
Three Diamonds (1991)
Mythologies of the Heart (1996)
No Respect: New & Selected Poems 1964–2000 (2001)

PHOTOGRAPHY

Screen Tests/A Diary, in collaboration with Andy Warhol (1967)
Six Portraits (1975)
Good Girls (1994)
Seizing the Moment (1997)
Resistance to Memory (1998)
Screen Tests Portraits Nudes 1964–1996 (2000)

SELECTED COMPILATIONS

Transatlantic Review #52—An Anthology of New American Poetry (1975)
Little Caesar #9/"Unprecedented Information" (1979)
Angus MacLise Checklist 1959–1979 (1981)
UP-TIGHT: The Velvet Underground Story (with Victor Bockris, (1983)
Scopophilia: The Love of Looking (1985)
A Purchase in the White Botanica: The Collected Poetry of Piero Heliczer
    (with Anselm Hollo, 2001)

COMPACT DISCS

48 Cameras & Gerard Malanga, Three Weeks with My Dog, Besides 006
    (1999)
Gerard Malanga, Up from the Archives, sub rosa SR170 (1999)

GERARD MALANGA

NO RESPECT

NEW & SELECTED POEMS 1964–2000

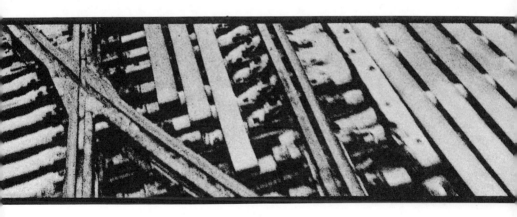

BLACK SPARROW PRESS
SANTA ROSA • 2001

ACKNOWLEDGMENTS

Grateful acknowledgment is made to the following publications in which some of the poems in Sections XII and XIII first appeared, sometimes in slightly different form: *Agni, Denver Quarterly, Ecstatic Peace Journal, episodic* (Paris), *Grand Street, Ignite, Pharos* (Paris), *Poetry, Prairie Schooner, Purple* (Paris), *Raritan, Southwest Review, Stand* (UK), *The Massachusetts Review, The Ohio Review, 21st: The Journal of Contemporary Photography, van Gogh's Ear* (Paris), *Verse* and *Willow Springs.*

Acknowledgment is also made to Pym-Randall Press for the poems comprising Section II, which appeared in *chic death,* copyright © 1971 by Gerard Malanga; to Great Lakes Books for *Prelude to International Velvet Debutante* comprising Section IV, copyright © 1967 by Gerard Malanga; to Black Sparrow Press for the poems comprising Sections V, X and XI, which appeared in *Ten Years After: The Selected Benedetta Poems* (1977), *Three Diamonds* (1991) and *Mythologies of the Heart* (1996) respectively; and to Gil and Deborah Williams for "The Journey," which first appeared in their Bellevue Press postcard series.

Section VII includes several poems which first appeared in *Sparrow 22,* July 1974, published by Black Sparrow Press.

The following anthologies are also acknowledged for poems making their first appearance in print:
> *Bear Crossings,* edited by Anne Newman and Julie Suk, The New South Company © 1978, for "We Go Out into the Night."
> *Ratio: 3 Media Shamans,* Series Editor: Words, Temple Press Ltd., © 1991, for "Eban."
> *Overtones diptychs and proportions* by Ralph Gibson, Edition Stemmle © 1998, for "L'Histoire de Paris."
> *Night Errands, How Poets Use Dreams,* edited by Roderick Townley, University of Pittsburgh Press © 1998, for "Morning of January 2, 1993."

Arranged in chronological sections, this book brings together almost 36 years of work.

Cover photograph by Gerard Malanga.

LIBRARY OF CONGRESS CATALOGING-IN-PUBLICATION DATA

Malanga, Gerard
   No respect : new & selected poems 1964–2000 / Gerard Malanga.
   p.   cm.
   ISBN 1-57423-162-6 (paperback)
   ISBN 1-57423-163-4 (cloth trade)
   ISBN 1-57423-164-2 (signed cloth)
   I. Title.
PS3563.A42 N62 2001
811'.54—dc   2001035145

for
Asako

present | future
future | present

Contents

No Respect

New & Selected Poems
1964–2000

I make alchemy in the only way that one can do it nowadays, that is without knowing it.

—Marcel Duchamp

2000

1990

1980

1970

I. The Fashion Poems
(previously unpublished)

1960

A Newly Discovered Fashion Poem

Here's balance: this
walking skirt and this easy-
fitting length of jacket
that stops just where the pleats break,
gives them room
to start swinging.

And here's balance: it runs
like an invisible cord,
right up the center of this lithe
body, straight all the way—ankles
through pelvis through head.
Held as it should be, directly
over the shoulders. Try it: use
your earrings as a guide; imagine
they're dangling
on the tendon just back of the neck.
You'll find you're moving your head
back a little,
shoulders a bit forward—and
balancing with ease.

Castel's, 14 rue de Princesse, Paris

Too many accusations under the stair
Case in the small room behind the small table.
Too many secrets let loose overseas.
I am restless with the only major sentiment in Paris.
The car crash keeps coming back
And receding inside the dream.

Though the footsteps in the dark are not heard
And the confusion of headlights
Crossing each other are not
Off in the eyes in the night,
Exposure keeps corrupting every lifeline.
The May issue of French *Vogue* carries a cover of Deborah Dixon.

The Yellow Slicker

Pensive, contemplative, the model
wears a man-tailored white shirt
with pants. In New York
the body of Pietro Lega, 72,
lies beneath a bus for 20 minutes.
The girl who lives in her times
is the girl who wears black
in summer, white in winter.
In Las Villas Province, Cuba,
a former Batista Maritime Police Chief
lies face down, and still bleeding,
moments after the firing
squad's signal to shoot.
This is called "Revolutionary justice."

To a Young Model, Name Unknown

(photographed by Francesco Scavullo)

The Peck & Peck Girl applauds
the strategy of a Hadley cashmere. Now
gentle country air (left)—to go calling
in the afternoon—pale gray flannel dress,
gracefully princess-shaped, its great collar,
deeply cut, filled with a fluff of gray rabbit fur.
The new country look of the jumpsuit (opposite)—
here, fresh, bright and Irish in white-stitched,
sheer navy blue wool; "Irish Country Airs"—
The changing outline of Irish fashion.

Chanel

It is less a reflection of a period
than an anticipation of it.
Little by little altering and perfecting
the image, making it,
incredibly, more luxurious,
more contemporary, more complete.
Always, the rigorous magic of
the total Chanel impact—
the glorious thick tweeds
with their easy jackets,
so correctly hung from flawless shoulders,
the impossibly fresh blouses,
the exquisite stitched-down
linings and the weight of gold chain;
the skirts with their lithe cloche-like
movement over the hips and the short
easy walking hems … the surprise of
the legs and feet in nude-looking
pink-beige stockings and slimp-pumps
to match, racing out—slim and sexy—
under the brawny tweeds—
the Chanel hair, round, ribboned
with thick, thick bangs.

Walking in the Rain

Left: Black jersey and streaks
from white lightning—
another by the foam
backed fabrics
firming up rain
coat-history now.
Small round collar, dolman sleeves.
In Ban-Lon jersey over DuPont nylon
(S. Edward fabric),
laminated in Fortezza
(of Scott Foam). About $200. Altman's;
Halle Bros.; Blum's, Chicago; L. S. Ayres.

The Model that Models for Buick '65 Buick

Clean, sleek, beautifully proportioned, the model
is just now beginning to be seen
at the most important events—
years younger—dramatic by the minute.

Provocative, beautiful, the long
neck and royal head; confident
the model leans with ease and grace
against the side—the chrome grilled in the sunlight.

II. *chic death,*
poems 1964–66
(published 1971)

2000

1990

1980

1970

1960

Now in Another Way

for Andy Warhol

Gradually it is the exultant cement factory that becomes us.
I am thinking that the hand trembles like the obsessive lumberyard of a
    phrase
As she stands confident beside the glamorous vending machine.
And as her mouth finds for itself a drinking fountain
Now in another way I become more involved with the uncontrolled
    climate of her breath
For as long a time as this poem lasts and lasts,
Like the difficult dawn of an arched eyebrow misplaced.
Now in another way pausing at the end of a paintbrush,
The artist is stretching and stapling as the determined look of somewhere
    ahead
Becomes two faces destroying themselves, that turn black with repetition.

The Pleasure Seekers

Our lives in these report cards are not heard.
Being so much at once at one time,
We never got used to "Calabria."
The shadows fell on the desk in blue squares.
At the pier the boat is made ready for the competition.
I am being thrown against the term "alternative."
What does it mean simply to persuade?
Then I collapse in the green car on the brown road.
My name is John or Bill
As the notebook is removed from the coat
Pocket and placed within hand's reach of the dashboard,
Keeping me safe in seats that were once comfortable.
The colors are causing carefully chosen combinations
Which I cannot understand, entirely.
They go on unnoticed except for the time
She had eaten too much.
The water was rough that day.
Signals were at once dispatched.
Everything was at land but the boat
Whose white sail settled into the waves,
Far from the safety of the shore.
Here and now I cannot remove this place
From the temperature
Changes and the plant growing, older, now.

Zucchini

What does it mean to be weightless as a tooth
Pick or to know the taste that brings on "great" value?
And the boisterous affection for which reprisal
Should not be taken seriously remains useful.
Without fear of "the cliff fiend" the flowers
Have proven forgiving, compassionate, and deadly.
We sit down to eat and need to get back
To something necessary and simple.
This passage should involve human eyes,
But it's even more impatient to avoid
A certain amount of impatience regarding
A system of values that would reduce "the storm."
"I should like to see you drive a car."
"Oh. Would you?!"
"Isn't this a kind of predictable dressing-up of
A poetic commonplace?"
"I don't know."
"One of my favorite flowers smells."
"The Burning Peninsula" has just been released.
The road is smoothly executed.

Burning Days

The current and a strong south wind
Brought them to the city by nightfall.
The missionary smiled as he
Handed him a letter. "My tongue
Is as dry as a stone in the desert,"
He said. Then courage whispered
Its orders. We hurried back
Toward the earthwork. The sky grew dark.

The missionary smiled as he
Brought them to the city by nightfall.
"Toward the earthwork the sky grew dark,"
He said. Then courage whispered
"The current, and a strong south wind
Is as dry as a stone in the desert."

Photos of an Artist as a Young Man

for Andy Warhol

He lies on bed—white walls
behind him:
furniture scarce.
Illustration of shoe
horn hangs on wall behind
and above him. He has
dark hair. He holds Siamese
cat in arms. It's 1959.

"I grew up in Pittsburgh
after the war: ate soft
boiled eggs every day for two years:
attended Carnegie Tech;
went to New York: lived
with ten dancers on the Upper West Side;
freelanced in shoe illustration
with I. Miller Shoe."

Beyond the slow introduction
to refinement, the development of character,
it's not easy to breathe. He is
the invisible and unimaginable journey
through colors silk-screened on canvas
what he or the boy may have seen
years before, standing there
in the field, young, innocent, speechless.

Silver Dracula

Sleep is what we find in waking.
This is sand to the legs
You the boy grass on hills.
We walk around in the back
Yard all year. So this is
The way out into the roads
Of the city. And the jar
On the shelf doesn't move
Nor resemble much. We get hungry.
Though I had never left
Across the other road
Was in progress for the demarcation,
"Demarcation." We make it some times of
The year. It was already killed by reading.

Comic-Strip

We drop our tablets into the glass of soda
Water. The emphasis is well worth remembering.
This is the breath of our satisfaction.
We are dwelling in a seaport
Not to be disturbed. We do not
Remove our shirts after the swim.
Now I'm in love with the nightmare of being famous.
You are standing beside the boat and it's raining.
We are doing something that I can't
Quite make out what it is,
But the flowers are whispering words
In black ink on white ground.
We call these "interceptions." We call these "balloons."
We remember the directions we chose
And the way in which we grew.
Now you proceed to pass me the lit cigarette,
As trees continue to bend in a wind
That has its source from the open sea
And meets its shore in the East,
Where the light comes in advance of the sun.

The Hyphenated Family / sonnet

Nothing disturbs so much as the logic of music:
Going far enough the waves that navigate the boat;
All my looks astride the way those Ford
       girls bend in the wind
Shield their hair funneling behind them
       in a biography of grass.
It's quiet here among the international
       set in the afternoon of this arm
Pit it was this pit that got caught between my teeth.

"He was dying. And he was my son," the fire
Man said. Then the life insurance got caught
       in the air
Shaft. By this the grace of the body is not qualified
       nor well
Done. The flowers painted black by friendships.
This is the will of an approaching member not to be
       touched:
The iridescence of oil on the surface of water,
       the canned rations, the drift
Wood. But now the chair is being pushed under
       the table.
There was not time for that at this
       far place in the night.

The Underbrush

for Virginia Harrison

We greet January head on with a dashing leather helmet.
But I didn't hear you when you said it.
The coloring book was opened to the blue page
And she was instructed to return.
This much I cannot defeat. The danger of
These sharp turns is transmuted into a danger
We try to avoid. The result is the windshield
Getting blurred with ice.
There is no reason to panic but we are at a complete loss.
Going back there I continue to go blind
making "right" turns in the wrong direction.
This means you are horrified to be part of the morning
When the miracle didn't occur but brought you
This far in the road's "authority" to lose sight
And the assurance of sleep.
We could not distinguish the surroundings
Nor the visitors who were instructed to leave.
We fell quietly into the rain
Storm and were helpless. Some thing
Less than all this became extremely important.
Thus you find this unforgiving, the relentless
Search for "the ones" responsible.
The drama continues on roadsides in various
Parts of "the country." This offers us
The illustrious future of the thruway.
What is that, burning?
I thought of not going home because
The "classification" was changed.
I was not bothered anymore.
My address is lost in the files of the Armed Forces
And only elegance seems the necessity by choice.
Yet here in this bed
Room I have forgotten my boyhood and the hairless bodies.
Living was no longer a problem and there is nothing to worry.
This, of course, presents a vacation.

Being injured found him at once strong and successful.
We've been here a short time who would have thought
So much at one time the storm shedding happiness among strangers.
What is the pause that refreshes? Or where the road sign disappears
All is not that beautiful or climactic.
This is the new realism we have arrived at.
Why is my hair trickling me this way?
Where did she go?
Now my anonymity is protected.
I have stopped eating and "First Aid" is only a memory.
It's impossible to force my way out of this burn.

New Art

for Andy Warhol

Of the sidewalk covered with blood
A light puts up signs—a road
A disc the music begins.
The night it began.
So is this car
Out into the roads of the city
Eastern shore
What we the speed
Energy that tribute was dazzling
That follow my eyes
I cannot move away from these paintings
Itself a decision that instinct makes
Choosing more that the machines
Can do. The day over the table
Disturbed in his lunch
He reaches for repetition
With which he'll be passive and safe.
Walls reflecting
Observe the crushing of fenders
Into concrete eyesight can't keep.

Though I had always come here
This factory
We make it several times of the year
The floors lined with sheen
The traffic still goes
We don't kill
And I am possessed
Of these terms in our lives we don't want.
The electric chair in a room made silent by signs
Over the door,
The flames coming toward us—
Accidents of some future date.
We sit on couches, but the sleep
And ideas persist

Knowing we gain from it,
To fall apart again.
Some simplicities first
Then nothing—night
The secret, visible late next day. Or next week.
On the telephone. The film.

Windshield

Now it is beginning and nobody knew it.
The auto accident continued to repeat itself
In the brochure and flowers were choking the air
For more sunlight. The demonstration of sleep
Had made him beautiful. A bibliography was offered.
The poem found its way into our headaches. In the boat
House we committed the action of sodomy
To drift across the floor
Boards and think of the bird who would not stay.
But the boat was firmly secured to the pier in need of repair.
What were we to be included into?
And did it rise into negative sky
Line?? Everything else floats in its own time
Machine. Now I am coming in and out of you
In dreams of corduroy. The clouds
Carefully included you into focus
Geared up for the big race. But who recovers
From the weight of the tornado fiend?
Everything was continuing continuing:
Headlights plunging into the dark
Further ahead was a bridge through which
There were the remains of miles of
Collisions we have missed, indicated by several road
Markings that were no longer specific.
But what here of we that they thought heard
Into our sleekest parts and the dream of
The dashboard, the continuing destination that was not theirs?
Sparks were coming from my hair. His name is John.
But now his name is no longer John,
Or was it Fred who exists in the clouds
In disguise yearning for the point from which
He took off, as if dying depended
On repetition and height in the fabulous dry
Turmoil of a long afternoon these sensations are making on him.
This keeps happening only once without encouragement,
Though it is only real to rise onto another unconditional surrender of air,
Leaving us at that and the body was not fractured nor bruised.

Fresh Death

We understand that machinery as we truly disturb
    the grass:
From every terminal in the right city
    at different times of the day
The water was cool that was something to the touch of hair.
But he continued to consult his *Traveler's Guide* about
The rest of the year. How can we be so precocious?
A cloud induced him by lighting in the wind's
    crippled reflection,
So goodness may plant itself in the burn.
Yet here on this island I have lost sight and sound of the new reality
And try to hear what they are saying out on the boat;
But it seems there is an intermission
In the newsreel's documentation of armies
Mingling with jungle and mud.
There's this network we just came from.
Now the wind of the winter increased and the young boy
Is lurking in the shadows of the public library
"Head." Of what they and all we are now know us.
But you heard after you began to lose us out
We lived before they went blind thinking us safe
These repetitions we think they are.
Fields lay down in his eye. The metal was sharp
Edged. But the trees push the explanation of
    their height
Into the darkness to live in peace.
What can the sun that moves all day across the sky
Line and over invisible borders?
What can the sun, what can the other road
Signs prove in the distance?
Who invents virtue and gives no one a look?
The blazing headache seemed pale among the weeds.
This is why the snake is eager for it must
Have motion and the snow though vague
Is soon gotten over. Perhaps
This collision too heads into the head of a

mysterious summons.
People come down to see the collision.
But it's already too late.
The witnesses have vanished.
The new reality had brought him what it seemed
He could understand what was meant as warning.
Might the dream not contain all that is real?
The rivers, the unavoidable accidents,
The careers of the dearly departed
Or carefully-planned explosions?
Presently the friends guard their memories;
The boat departs for its seasonal cruise
In the Caribbean and back into winter.
He thought then of the fire
Man holding a child in his arms
Thirty times till his face and his arms and the child
Are all undefined, as if the paint tore up, the figures
Dissolving in water and smoke.
I am not offered every good thing that I want.
This is monumental. This is tragic.
All attitude is engendered to be more subject, more large.
The road breathless and the eyes charmed by
The onrushing headlights going out into morning.
        The hands gone
To sleep at the steering wheel.
That's how he came nearer to what he was moving towards
In which we can only imagine a world of black clouds
And he walks away.
But what false secrets did the thermo-fax hold?
In the car's speed or did the nerves dissolve?
Dreams give fullness to our lives.
And now the men come to clean up the last of us.

The Circle Pins

Many distractions be eaten up
All the same games, the
We got bored with becoming same people.
Everything New York. This is where the talk, the minds, are in
Have too much of it. You the ideas are, but you can
The week the success bit, the press too involved in that scenery
Danger of trying to gear sure of making it big, the
Instead of doing it toward being successful
Disciplined, and it's very on my own.
The first hard for me to get
Working, and I was year we were married
To despise myself.
I have never been so depressed.
Can't do it, just live off someone else.
It's fun, in the city, success is
Many doors open for you
Serious women who are driving force.
Artistic—they might start slightly talented, slightly
Bands because they lack taking it out
On their too much for their own focus.
There, ambition is to take out their frustrations'
Sense of worth. And they come
A cancer. Everyone has been because there is so much
Pleasure in idleness. But he squeezes you
In New York, everything moving a sense of.
Now calling of yourself he squeezes you
In to be idle this thing I am working.
It is as I am, even inching along.
Much the presence of the actually, it is not so
Professional standards that "top," and the city's strictly
From getting started, but keep some "pit"
Because she is afraid, young men, after all,
Are piano jobs available to her?
In fact that they may not not similarly dissuaded by the fact is City
Begins to feel anything at all a part of "the action"
In the city from small towns. Women who come to

For a girl to be, and if were "there is one single
To do something besides you"
Were bright and wanted to get out or change to fit just
Was one single ladder of the rest—towns where the
For anyone "different"—success and no room on it
Which lets them. So many are escaping
Of values to uphold the conformity to continue.
Who simply had to have some?
So now she's running this place to use her talents.
At Sardi's afterwards the way we go.
Into this world and the machinery of rain.

The Hotel Speaks

The pavilion physique
Seen poised let told rose
Celery fate wound tree lent fur
Dome mass two doors debut the run let flame knew
Don't less shave you glisten come or mention the hombre
        sir in revery worn a auto detriment
Fast marbles save saints entrainment piece key jungle
An excess roscus
Messy crayons soluble circulars
Excess collage that veered
Lot entrance desk quells blew it on seal or compass
In souvenir day potent imitable
Maintenance lay nodge jar dream pass lard petite loan
        convenience assets or
Veal couped in phlegm or bust magic axe yes palm
Incestuous lure beau real grand air intelligence
Satire competent injury
Dale Autry coat plus cab sir less bull dune grandville
Items billiard avest des trains day sole sir furs rug
        are diabolo this tempt ancient
Less jambles moose nodge fruit tiers mount the torn day lot sir
On apricot plus quinine main trees blanched
Let poles west figure part duck minus station allies
Balanced in absence us sill enter less quart must
Defendent met wheat
Does shopping bands day rose key front assault the garage
Jessica see the eclipse orient itself
Turn boys or find the masses
Decode equal at or all axe shapes color decay
Flaw night bowls day rage
Less gridirons charm mats less lack cares motes pass tender maid
Don't Autry pore on home bazaars
And obscure signalism to rest.

Temperature

When the sun shone hot the girl's arm was detected
       by the temperature changes, either by a drop
       when the girl walked into his shadow,
or by a rise when the sun shone upon her
       as she neared the sun. The sun also became
       part of love's odors which could be detected.

It was odorless indoors, but the arm
       gave off a distinct taste of lemon like the sun
       when the sun struck the edge
of the girl's arm out-of-doors.
       He could tell by the sense of smell
       and the temperature changes alone when he was near her.

On a cloudy day, or when the sun was just a sun,
       the girl's arm was lacking his attention.
       The boy was also lacking on a cloudy day,
but the recess of the sun behind his head
       did not immediately bring about a cessation of the odor,
       or the temperature changes on the girl, from the sun.

Any of these temperature changes was at times sufficient
       for the perception of the girl. Like a blindman,
       the boy grasped at the odors that would serve him.
Though the odors from the wind, or the arm,
       and the sun were at times sufficient, they
       were neither necessary nor always present.

Skis

A girl, her profile important,
distinctive, stands in silhouette
holding skis, wearing goggles:
the warm winter sun
light fixed behind her
head; the sky imitating the sea.

I struggle against my own vindictive providence;
but she is like the Etruscan who sort of
feels the land by walking
on it for weeks at a time.
I don't see her nor where
the light, at night, of something
coming toward me thru the snow.

The Long Shirt

This is the weight of the body tilted
on the right leg, the head
thrown back, and to the left,
the neck, long-stemmed,
provocatively exposed—
the model stands erect—closely set
apart from sand and sun
light, lightly enclosed in a long shirt,
the shape gracefully narrowed
over the bust; the skirt,
widened by gores; the sleeves
funneling freely.

Natural Good Looks

They don't expect to have the looks
they plan for faces
replace the going face,
to express the clothes
they wear; to close
the head in, to emphasize
the eye, wash out the face, the eye
brows to a fine line
until they almost disappeared
into the skin
cream officially recognized.

Tripod

Another three minutes passed without moving,
Followed by flashes and flares,
Sprocket holes time-lapsed by compositive printing.
The moth stopped rising on the arm of the chair
And somehow the technical terms are not encouraged
To be read on the long summer nights
When friends neglect to greet one another.
Life pursued up these hills
In the book. Today, of course, it is time
To go elsewhere, outlining the tree
To such advantage as to prove
Slightly commercial and the sun
Light in the square makes everything round.
In a moment the film would be placed in the can.

SIZE 8
HEIGHT 5'7"
BUST 34
WAIST 22
HIPS 33½
—THE FORDS

Pinstripe

(from a photo by Francesco Scavullo)

for Beate Schultz

Headlights hitting the eyes
Thru the wind
Shield, a new day is beginning
What was out there in the sun
Light because it's August.

Though a girl walks, her back
Bare, down a road which ends
When she passes the fence
Into the field, there's already
An impulse to be
Wherever she goes,
Pointing north of the knee.

Coming Up for Air

for Edie Sedgwick

The face that grows out from the magazine
Covers some simple indication
That long earrings are coming
Back into fashion
At the parties that were
Beginning over
Night in the city
Limits, and the surprise
Package of whatever explains the false
Hood of logic to keep us
Guessing at the eventual sun
Rise, brings me home
In the film of our favorite soft
Drink starring you.

The Tranquil Tub

for Alexandra Kirkland

It is day. I am awake, and the atmosphere
Is electric. The window is left open
Because of some simple contradiction.
But the choice of colors and sophistication
For social events is unlimited.
Activities will include friends' debuts,
Dinner parties, charity balls. Outside
A white tree in silhouette, far
Off, behind, the window which tries
To conceal it; a jet glides silently
Across the sky. There is only
The torrid truth of a two o'clock sun,
Only the hair floating on the water's surface.

The Young Mod

for Jean Shrimpton

The model, vigorous, attractive, modern, is for
touring the tennis courts and terraces
in a two-piece ensemble of weightless
naked wool. The dress a clean white sleeveless
sweep of shape, with its own double
breasted jacket; it will never show
signs of travel fatigue. The port shelters
a sleek assemblage of yachts. But she
is leaving the race with the clock to others
and forgetting the crowds and confusion.
The naked wool bolero-back skimmer
is just the sort of almost-nothing weight
she'll need for sun and sea. A man lies
dead along the wreckage of his auto.
Another is still pinned behind the steering wheel.

III. **The Debbie High School**
Dropout Poems
(previously unpublished)

2000

1990

1980

1970

1960

Empty Lives

The friend asks me to pull the garrison
Buckle, to loosen the belt
On the arm. I see
The "good looks" evaporate
In my dream to survive with
Or without them or her.
A third person is sleeping
In the back room,
Complicating matters
About where I can stay tonight,
And there is no end to inquiry.
The faces are all very still.
Nobody's about
To say anything personal, new.

But why must they always
Annihilate something
Beautiful in themselves
By misunderstanding my good
Intentions to help them look
After themselves?
Who stashed the works
And where did she put them?
And is shooting up a substitute,
After all, for sex between new acquaintances?
Is the flower
Pattern that smells
Lovely? Is it some childish scheme that is taking
Place if I stand
Still for a moment thinking of the day
Breaks they will eventually lose?
And whose is that turtleneck jersey she's wearing?

I don't know what's mine until I've thrown it away.

—Rene Ricard

Rene Ricard Is Twenty at Nineteen

There's no light in that carload of friends
And the remembrance of things past
Forgetting who he is is not early
Morning in the small room
Filled with cunning tots
He surrounds himself with.

Whatever happened to smart conversation?
Why did he stand
Up to the messy lives in the diary
Notebook to be read as one makes it
Several times of the week
And who is the young boy smiling in the photo machine?

He drops in and out of their lives,
For it's not easy to decide where he's
Going out every night
Because there's nothing of interest
For him to hold their attention long enough,
Though he did not know them three months ago.

Catalyst

The purpose of friendships is inconsistent.
This is the story of my life
Creating friends' myths for them
And later finding myself
Bereft of anything meaningful.
The other friends are flying
Off into the death
Masks necessary among the small
Rooms; but the gossip consistently spreads
For days. It seems perfectly natural—
The young girl who sleeps
For two days—the same girl who stays
Awake three and a half nights in a row.

Destinations

The amphetamine rapture!
And her skin is white
As a ghost is white sometimes,
In our dreams—
As white as a vial of white powder.

This month's allowance is due.
She'd better comb her hair to look
Well, though she's not too cool,
Keeping Ondine around for the inexhaustible
Source of supply:
The white powder sniffed off
The flat edge of a knife, plate glass,
A piece of tinfoil.
She's there in the backroom
Flat on her back. She drops
Out in my life.
How the parasites love her.
It's the torn bags of garbage I have to get
Across some Lower East Side address or other.

Finding Our Way Back at Night

Through our birthdays sometimes a horse roams
Across the open
Field, where sometimes we're
Found sitting behind the small rocks
Discussing my film
Projects. The long dream of childhood is not shameful
And my throat is not dry.
What are you doing there
In the wardrobe closet?
Why are you in love with your school
Master? The "factory" made those
Paintings superb. Your class
Mates appear much younger
Wishing you "good wishes."
Debbie, please wake up!

"I Missed You by Only Two Blocks"
—Debbie

On the hill
This boy comes back
You read about it
Those blue eyes
In the darkness
The foul intelligence
I am happy
To state.
Would you like your picture
Taken? Is devotion painful
In broad daylight? Let's go
Outside where I stand
Upside down in the film
To be developed for compositive printing.

The source to her
Problems cannot be traced,
Yet I don't understand the wisdom of remaining
Silent. Breaking out in a cold
Sweat is not always wise.

Notes are dropped
Out in
The envelope that have something
Or nothing to do with me.
The friends take
Part in the empty room.
Tell me where to sleep.

The Leaves

I dream the dream that you dream of,
Although she can't
See me walking towards her
Close friend with the soft impression of the white rose
Plot in my hand
Because she takes
Part in the gathering of staying
Up nights when it's raining.

But I see other friends
That she speaks of
When she also sees
Sitting in the small room
When daybreak is
Approaching with the promise of sunlight.

Trees are the aroused emotions of the earth. The prevailing winds pile up the dunes.

—*Angus MacLise*

Exercise in Excess

Trees are the aroused emotions of the earth,
The prevailing winds pile up
The dunes, and yet the chance is not more
Complete than ever before to include the light
Switch preceded by solitude.
Thus there was time for all projects
To come to the surface into something that matters.
The moment of modern
Living is always present, though the vanishing
Point towards the terrible blatant daydream
Because we go to the seashore
As authorities of the limp frame of the female
Body, cosmic efforts reduced to the open
Dream structure traced with looking concern.
We have already begun our lives as foretold,
Tumbling upward on the front
Page of the morning
Edition, freedom so often
The way we respond to anyone's thinking.
It's not easy to forget the cosmic efforts.
It's not easy to forget the cloudbursts
Intruding everywhere, the acres of weeds
Transformed into the immense journey of daylight
Falling over your left shoulder.
This presupposes the topic to be re-examined
In spite of the romantic spirit proving to be
Deadly sometimes.
Clouds did not move off the torn
Page in the child's dream of eternal living
Conditions. A breath of fresh air
Raids continued to move in the room
Through the open window.

That the young girl could
Sit and do nothing means
She would remember her friends.
All that ever came of it was growing
Up without ever returning to the small room,
Almost tragic in the dismal twilight.

Water with Bloodstains in a Glass

for George Millaway

This was the way into the wine
Cellar and out of the trip
Book water with blood
Stains in a glass, the medicine
Cabinet the friends looked at
This year; that phone
Call uptown, the sun
Light moving over itself in the water
Mark. What I want
To do is talk about the friendships,
How ripoffs are playing
An important part in their lives.
The dream of what we see inside
The small room is not
The dream book to have color
Placed into the blank spaces,
Though Rene stands beside the white tree in the moon
Light which doesn't move
And Debbie is lost
In the thoughts of her diary dreambook
Entries raising suspicions, actions to be judged later.
The friends are unable to start
Until they start in the day
Light that commends them to open
The window, walk through the weeds
Reaching more weeds, to turn on
The flashlight to stand for awhile
Without moving in the dream
Of the living
Expense the friends cannot compensate
For the sole purpose of seeing them
Shoot themselves up, so that
Anxiety accumulates into unspoken careers.

Drugs and Cosmetics

Day expires on the glass
Above the sink. The sun
Light fades from red to purple.
When the young girl has time
She has freedom.
But whom do the friends attribute
Their activities and emotions to
And why are they not free
From oral obligations, principles?
19 Eighth Avenue is a dream.
Around the rooms friends
Whom you don't know, not saying much. A cold
Light scatters powder on the plate
Measured by the stainless steel
Knife. The friends anxiously await to get in.
The young girl's tortured
Attempts to deal with the problem in her trip
Book diary is the dream of the girl's loose
Leaf pleats blowing about the legs.
The young boy searches for simple answers
For his friends who don't understand what he's
Saying. The relationship between the swapped
Destinies is a personal reality.
The young girl is sitting on the fire
Escape not thinking.
So many lives are cut
Short in the dream of the diary
Entry to be painstakingly revealed.
One gets used to
Not saying anything. One gets in
The way around the room is through the door.
One dies of thirst and ambition.
One dies of staying too long in one position.
Friends take
Advantage of your confusion.
Nobody knows the moment when the eye

Dropper is needed.
There are rumors of noise without reason and in my mind
There are names and living faces.
The young girl sets up love against
Life in the small room that the dead
Dream of the low-living share.
We are not sad together.
Sometimes I don't see you
Behind me. Fatigue of relaxing will
Assume the break
Down where they sit, not saying a word.
There is a world of things
To do in the rising sun
Light when we rub our eyes.
I walk with you. I stop
You are young.
"Trembling I hang by a thread;
I cease to exist if no one thinks of me," you said.

2000

1990

1980

1970

**IV. Prelude to International
Velvet Debutante**
(published 1967)

1960

Prelude to International Velvet Debutante

You walk out on the lawn.
The rising sunlight above you
Filters through the nearby trees.
Clouds are reflected in the water
Fountain. The grass is warm.
The estate is empty and you are
Alone lying on your back quietly.
You have bookings to meet
And your first month's rent is paid for.
This is your pale summertime
To learn history, to fill your closets
With new fashions for Fall.

o

You see friends you can never see
Again. Your face is pressed to the window pane
And it is raining. You are standing
In the center of the room
Wearing a see-through evening gown.
Your place the book upon the table.
You are standing on the hill.
Storm clouds accumulate. It's getting dark.
The road leads outward.
You are thinking of Rene
Who's in New York.
Chase has left for Maine.
You are looking for a place to stay.
You have graduated this year
From finishing school.
The opportunities for your future are limitless.
You open the door and walk
Out into the street
Walker's dream of the future
State of the sun
Light behind you

In the billboard drinking a Coke.
Today you buy Fabergé Evening Eyelashes.
The large room is painted white.
You may show up at the *Arthur* at any hour.
The phone calls are annoying.
The car crash cannot be forgotten.
You go to Stewart Agency for an interview
And you are not accepted.
You eat half a grapefruit.
Rene is safe in New York;
But without a place to stay at the moment.
You have not made reservations for the shuttle
Flight to New York.
It is late
Afternoon. Ed is sleeping
Andy's film projects are falling through.
There is no one out on the street.
Goodie is studying for his Italian course.
You are at home with your parents in Wellesley,
You are going out on a formal
Date tonight. Someone brings the *Times* to Gordon at
     Grolier.
Delmore Schwartz is dead at 52.
Lou Reed is out of the hospital, living
On East 3rd, Debbie's old flat.
You are applying your eye makeup with ease.
Real clouds fill the sky.
Sometimes you see your friends.
Sometimes you lose your sandal in the car.
You appear on the cover of *Mademoiselle* at seventeen.
The real dream becomes a nightmare.
You stand near quicksand
In a little girl dress.
You step out of the limousine,
Days of 1966 ahead for you:
You will protect Rene.
You are everywhere beside the rocks
In the silhouette swimsuit
Caught on an Italian holiday

By John Palmer's camera.
The place is Portofino.
A narrow, winding street, streaming
Sunlight, and admiring glances
From a happy girl having a wonderful time.
Somehow, wherever you go
You seem to be the center of attention.
Your relaxed, informal personality radiates
Warmth. Perhaps, it's your inner confidence that shows,
Shows in your walk, in the way you smile,
And in that special look that you have
When you know you look
Your best. You can't break away
Fast enough on the beach
When you've a trouser
Suit to show off in.
There's no particular brand with everything
You need for the look of the moment.

o

You are the first great post-atomic breakthrough
Leader in make-up.
You are the most confident walking
From the crowded beach to water's edge.
You make sure that the bust
Outline remains constant when the straps are dropped
For sunbathing. You sport a new pale blue denim
Shirt with button-down collar and pocket on sleeve.

o

You are thinking of the tall boy you walked away from
This afternoon. Boston is behind
You for the summer; time to rearrange your living
Quarters in New York; to go on
"Go-sees"; eat little; go out
Dancing every night.
The changing landscape changes the local stops pass by.
You make a list of all the things you have

To do. You study the new scenario.
But you can't make up your mind.
You go back to your room.
Destinies are pronounced in the month's fashion
Magazines. Libra is your sign and for June
At various times throughout the month the Sun,
Mars, Mercury, and Venus all make
Harmonious aspects to your Sun sign.
The last three are all small planets and their effect is
Sudden and transitory. Foreign
Interests loom large and even
Extended travel can be undertaken.
However, a word of warning
About physical mishaps:
It is time for safety
Precautions. Don't ignore small health
Problems. Neptune in your house of Personal
Finances still adds a sort of illusory influence to your money
Matters and you may have to wait
Till the end of the month
Before your finances improve.
Most Librans will be experiencing some exceptionally good
Opportunities in their careers.
Between now and the end of September.
Jupiter transits your solar tenth house,
Ruled by Cancer, and it should be a fashion period for all
Matters connected with your professional life.
You will get support from many unexpected sources
And there will be very few Librans who do
Not experience some form of advancement.
During the whole of June the planet
Mars is in Gemini, your House of Travel,
And it is heavily afflicted around the 20th and 25th,
So if possible, postpone any travel plans.

o

It's Sunday. You write long letters.
There's no work for summer.

Rene steals flowers from gardens for you.
Later, his friends will find him for you to take
Care of. And you polish his shoes and show
Your affection in many small ways.
You must return before morning.
You fall on the open field,
Grass shoots up around you.
You are in the *Arthur* with flowers placed in your hair.
You are concerned about the clothes you wear
Out of boredom and genuine need to have.
Something happens trapped in so much color;
Spring transformed into a dress or pants suit
You arrive with friends at the most
Unexpected places. All the parties that were
Were not important for you to attend. The jewels
You wear catch the rising sunlight.
Rene abuses you, sometimes;
He sometimes means to,
Sometimes not,
And the tragic fault lies in himself
To be ignored or abused.
You wake up at dawn and walk with the light
In a long, diaphanous gown.
The tall weeds are precious.
The animals are asleep, or hiding.
You are thinking about everything
You said about two minutes ago.
You run into the bathroom.
You sit alone in the air-conditioned apartment.
Thinking about ungrateful you will be to Rene.
Frank O'Hara is dead in the *News*.
You feel guilty for your behavior
Towards Mary. Andy takes you to the *Arthur*
For drinks. He has great plans for you.
He gives you advice.
Rene went off somewhere and has
Not called. You have moved
Into your room at the Chelsea.
The room is small but offers French

Doors and a balcony.
Your father returns to Boston.
You have to meet
Your first booking assignment.

o

You spray your Tom Collins in Rene's face
For fun at Max's Kansas City. You are going to wash
Your hair. Anthony Senna has got
The Boston Police threatening Rene's friends.
Ingrid has written some new poems
In her Trip Book.
Stewart Agency tells you to dye your hair
Blond and have the small moles on your cheek removed.
You wonder what Andy is doing
Tonight and you are upset with
The fact that you will be receiving
$300 a month to live on, which will
Include paying for hotel expenses,
Food and miscellaneous listings,
When before, when you were a student
At a posh boarding school,
You would receive $100-per-week
Allowance for clothes.

o

You slept a lot today.
You meet Debbie for the first time
On the 7th floor of the Chelsea.
Andy is waiting with friends at George Millaway's apt.
On West 3rd Street. You are dancing
At the Cinderella Bar.
You are thinking of Rene and what he's doing this very minute.
You would like to see him apologize
For the scene each of you caused at El Mio.
19 Eighth Avenue comes into your life.
Rene cannot lift his head from the pillow

To face you, and your back is to him.
He says a few words, speaks of Vivian Kurz's future
Read from the Tarot cards, and of his own destiny.
It is almost 5:00 A.M.
You take a cab back to the hotel
You are silent; but you are
Also crying. You wash your face.
You haven't slept in two days.
You forgot to take the birth control pill
Edie secured for you as a favor to me.

o

You owe Ingrid $2.50 and she said she would
Come by to cash the check at the hotel desk.
But she is two hours late.
You put off calling your father
Long distance to ask for an advance
On your $300-a-month allowance,
Even though he has offered to send you money
For the wardrobe you laid out your own money for.
You get up late every day and are in
Need of a rest. You do not get
Enough sleep. You have certain
Selfish qualities, also, but you're young.
Rene is positive and negative at all times.
He can get on people's nerves.

o

You put down drugs, but constantly rely on
Diet pills to keep you going
Thru the entire day.
Rene calls and you give
Into his wants. You play
Small games with your former boyfriends.
You cannot recognize your own affectations;
But you'd never admit to it.
Your new name will be mentioned

By Leonard Lyons, in his column, because
He likes your new name "International Velvet."

o

You scream into the telephone at Billy
Who hangs the phone up
On you, and you deserve it.
You want revenge.
What you really want is recognition.
Personal attention.
You have this compulsion to drive
Yourself right into the ground.
You don't want to sleep. It's 4:00 A.M.
Rene calls you and insists you come down to 3rd Street.
You decide you will.
You end up in bed with Lou Reed.
You're a very convincing liar
But you can't count on your friends to keep
A secret. The next day everybody knows of your childish
        pranks.
You write a letter to Daddy.
Filling it with lies, for example:
"I have thus arrived at the decision
With Andy's help that no one will be
Allowed to visit me without a specific invitation.
Also, Rene is no longer allowed in my apartment,
Nor is he considered a friend of mine.
He has insulted and embarrassed my friends,
Taken advantage of me by eating all my food
And considering my apartment open to him at all times.
I find this, to say the very least, very upsetting."
You destroy old relationships and make new ones.
Your name is mentioned in Leonard Lyons' column.

o

You receive a check from Daddy today
To cover your last week's clothing expenses.

Rene is no longer staying with you at the Chelsea.
Last heard from, he has taken some sleeping pills,
And it is rumored that he is not 20 but 28.
The Boston Police are still looking for him.
Your contactsheet is ready at the photo lab.
And you will be going to see Bea Feitler at *Bazaar.*
Last night you became extremely upset
Because someone at the dinner table at El Quijote had compared
You with Nico.
You went up to your apartment
Crying.

o

The new consciousness disappears with the moon
Where only the stars are coming out.
You have hopes to make money in London or New York.
Early afternoons you stand perilously on a ledge
For photographers and have no worries.
At night you are at the discotheque.

o

The trees have remained simple
Italian dragonfly trees.

o

Now you are free in a shapeless wind.
You find a place in the crowd where you see everything.
Several cities are on the ground
All of which you've been guided to the sounds familiar to your ears.
But when it is clear you will move
With your fur at your wrists and around your long graceful neck.
It's raining.

o

It's a good thing you come from Wellesley.
You are not alone in the morning
Papers. You walk towards home.
You would rather ride in a chauffeured limousine.
Today you walk through New York, unrestrained and possessed.
Here you are on the bed at some party
"Making it" with a young man who has
No intentions of seeing you again.
It is the end of night.
And in spite of you, I am revealing
Secrets you know nothing about.

August 1966. Hotel Chelsea, New York City

2000

1990

1980

1970

V. Ten Years After
(published 1977)

1960

Screen Test 3

Are the relationships between the swapped destinies
what light does on the torn page of the italicized text?
Then, do we inquire into the nature of the good
looks, since knowledge is a word embracing
numerous different kinds of statements and claims?
Efficacious grace is followed by the effect for which it is
intended and the friends are capable of occupying
space whom we attribute our activities and emotions
for reasons which function
beyond their inherent limits.
Perhaps it isn't the same thing as explaining
what involves our presence,
which involves the rain falling, which
involves inexhaustive repetition. Nevertheless
immortality of the soul is a gift and not intrinsic.

Waiting to Hear from You

Today my dream of you puts me
In orbit for some time to learn the truth
About the promise to phone
I wait to receive for some time.
The help around you is what you deserve
To take an interest in simplicity and grace;
But it's difficult for the young boy to avoid
Thinking of you. Long hair let
Loose shows an obsession with the wind
Breaker's dream of what light's thrown on
The ground. This is the light from heaven
Becomes visible in hands reaching out
With the promise to provide for
All the time you will be seeing me
Home. For the most part that was
Last weekend. I am thinking of you.

Dropping Out

Can we erase our lives from the lives
Who surround us in trip books and begin over again?
We see each other
Because we're not certain of seeing
Each other every day in the week
I record in the day-to-day entry.
The sunlight is repeating the fire
Escaping behind us in secret.
You pose and you twist and
You stand still in the shimmering landscape.
You perpetuate the various inspirations in my life
All about you. And you are
The only dream I ever desired to come true.

Schedules

Where was her presence in all of this
That's not fiction? And how does waiting have
Anything to do with the same way
It's painful for me to explain
Why you're not on
Time when I see you
Standing in weeds that come up
To your waist? I'm trying to imagine
The sunlight behind your head
Three months from now when the friends interrupt
Our life story in the snow
Storm living from books.
Sometimes I have to spend
An entire day deciding where I will be
Staying tonight.

The Photo Machine

The day begins with eternity
And we care
Enough through the storm
Windows breaking
Out loud, though this seems
Longer to transcribe the tape
Recording your voice:
ora ti Souvo un
Italiano, Ciao
Come stoi chi sei
tu e dove vai
non importa
Ceao Cè rumore qui
e non posso
dirti nulla.
Finally the photo machine frightens you
With its green light
And you look for yourself the way you looked
As a child in the "4 for a quarter" photos
Taken today. Actually you are the context of the young
Boy's inspiration you somewhat admit to
The light flashing behind your head
Pressed against his left shoulder is a still-portrait.

Getting Home Early

I looked for you
All over America
In the high-fashion ads.
Today you watched the rain fall from Penn's studio
Window overlooking Bryant Park.
I was writing poems and thinking of you
In the transparent universe
In the dull light of the afternoon dream cycle.
The genius of Dante's dream cycle is not past
Forgetting to whom his sentiments were meant for.
You drive off in the taillight's stop
Motion effect thru the rain falling.
You are my thoughts in the night
When I sit in the small room without you.

Sunday Evening

You are standing all over the landscape.
When I see the light dispersed through the clouds
Who explains these formations for me?
What is the meaning of heaven?

She remembers her childhood.
She remembers her father.
There were foreign schools to attend.
Now full-color covers cover your life in all the big cities:
Novita, the French and Italian editions of *Vogue*,
Issues now out-of-print.
But we are based on the new year of
Something entering our lives for the first time
Forever. I write about you in my diary notebook:
"Today not much happened"
The blood shifting in my head in the sunlight all afternoon.
You, somewhere in Connecticut.
The close friends forget
They don't really know you.
And you rise from the weeds in my dream
About you. I am examining my life story
In terms of how you fit
In, the temperature rising, also, seeing you always get
Out of the car to lock the door on my side.
Grace is going on into our lives because you know.
The snowstorm is melting away.

Further Discoveries

That yellow roses are a matter of life
And death is only understood
If we have confidence in living.

She started on her round-the-world
Dream of success in the open
Streets of Rome.

"Would you like to be photographed for *Vogue*?"

Simplicity and grace return
To be subsequently near us.

"I remember as a child hearing some bombs
Explode near my family's house by the sea
But they would always miss us, somehow."

The young boy with the rose
At the edge of the lake
Waits.

We have invaded each other's lives with
The one thing that has been able to save us
Since we were fourteen years old.

The Landscape Filled with the Grace of Your Posture

The dreams took us
By surprise. We knew
The wild flowers. We were discovering sunlight
Refracted in water. How to invade
The privacy of your day
Dream by the closed window.
The landscape fills with the grace of your posture:
The poem field rising in mist.
The experience of giving you these
Flowers to take home, the old and the new ones together.
I am not near you where we want to be, sometimes.
I am weary as I enter
The small room to sleep.

Benedetta's Room

Something sanctified in the way
Grace enters her life
As rain changing to snow
Falling on our heads in the twilight
Outlining the field
You stand in the open
Until the truth is explained
In the square
Sunlight all day.
The first memory of the imagination remains
Of yourself sitting
For three minutes in silence.
A page folded not to lose
My place in your life I write about
You. In a moment sunlight would
Fall through the window.

The Young Girl Moving Through Sunlight

The literature ending the very beginning of your life
Story is a release from my own.
Even as I think of you you are
Arranging the old and new flowers together.
All of this begins somewhere else.
Beatrice observed by Dante walking across
The *Ponte Vecchio*. What was he
Thinking? What are you...?
In the street by yourself.
In the car going home?

Hotel Chelsea, Room 121

for John Weiners

We wake up
In the sunlight pointing to the disadvantages of being up
Tight in the room making calls to friends
At the same time removing ourselves from
Broken promises.
John rolls a joint and thinks
About what time the mail is due to arrive.
Rene wraps himself up in a bedsheet.
Benedetta calls to let me
Know when to call her tonight.
Can't get thru to Andy today.
Today inspiration is lacking from my life.
Benedetta moves gracefully over the landscape into my life
With devotion and speed
Knowing where we are coming
From the moment we began
Somewhere inside.

I was living on a lonely part of the coast
of Tuscany, near Porto Santo Stefano. Allied Bombers
rained bombs on us night and day.

—Luigi Barzini
from The Italians

A Christmas Story

If only there was time to catch
Your breath. If only it were not
Hard to convey what you're hiding.

The friends that came with us this far have turned
Back.

Her father said, when she was fourteen,
"You can have it this way."

"100 years have passed," you said.

I have no other life
Story. Somewhere the light begins
To rise up behind your head, Benedetta.

What can she do with the wind in her hair.
With smart conversation at a government dinner?

Everyone is in black
Tie. The tall girl walks into the large room.
What is she thinking?
The rating game is a lie.

Promises of life in the Dodge Dart

In place of the radio
Music she keeps
Out.

Sunlight coming through
the bedroom
Window in Cambridge.

You can still hear Allied bombs fall nearby in your life
Line without changing target.

There is no snow on the ground.

Giotto di Bondone

The roadsign reads
Milano to Rome
On a crowded bus:
The child is found
Lost on a stranger's knee
By her father.
Today the tangible sense of form on her
Face making money for her is in
Transit. Purple and grey
Colors of normal emotions
Under observation
Her hand held
Tightly in mine.
Her head above water.

The past is infinitely better than the present, and that the future should reproduce the past.

—Nicolo Tucci
from Letter from Tucci

a handbook reference to flowers

Is venation the lifeline
Of the name that is hard to read on
The *envelope,* the sagittate leaf which opens
To the light and air in the small room?

Dreams of full color-plate reproductions
Explode on the white page in the light
Belt entering the young girl's room
The *general* and *horse shoe*
Spreads out of my immediate future
Fortune walking around New York City
In the late afternoon.

What sort of man, then, was Folco Portinari
About whom we know nothing?

One by one the lives are defined.
The imagination has no tradition to give it life
And the truth serum
Falls at our feet in the open field
On fire, the exciting detail of the joy ride
In detail, the decisions, the indecisions of Benedetta.
The absence of Laura's husband from her life.

The impulse to wait is possible and difficult
Looking helplessly for clues
To whom they wait still exist
Not in reach of the heart
Condition lacking compassion.

Will the waiting take

Time off her mind
Until Laura of *Firenze* comes home
Every night the way Benedetta waits
Up for her to? Is their reality of the
World without love
As real as my memory of them waiting
For someone to come?

The dreams speak to her in my life:
Venice. Rome, Montevideo, the City of New York;
Her life is trouble and doubt,
The spectrum of her birthday
Is not infinite
Because it does not fall on
The cusp.

Now I see the wisdom of the father for his son
In diplomacy—an "open" letter about
Table manners, wild flowers, knowledge.
I see the photo of a father and daughter
In Rome in the pages of *Life*
He neglected to see for so many years.
"We are in two different worlds"
She said. leaning forward
In the black-and-white photo
Machine.

Dreams of Benedetta Barzini of Porto Santo Stefano in the
    year 1966.
But now the dignity of love
Taken and given exits
As I told you the *annual* flowers in the end
Spring from the seed,
Make their full growth,
And die in one year.

In Search of America

The end of the world is beautiful today
Children clinging to their mothers
I see Veronica's cloth on fire
The friends give up
The hope of finding me happy
I've been looking for you for a long time
Wind vibrating trees
Can the young girl stand on her head
In the gym? Are the grateful dead
In the dream fire is on her
Face in the heart
"Benedetta, tell me, are we very
Far from Porto Santo Stefano?"
I feel sick
Death in Milano
1966
The indoctrination of crystal
Tears in the body
Line the mind the brain cells on fire
The *Navarro* intimately bound
Up with her childhood
Lycée Français de New York
The mother with the glass eye
The Dodge Dart
Rear signal light on a dark street
Blood on the bedsheet
You wake up to the alarm set for 8:30
The literature of high fashion
Fatigues you can't escape from
Turning in all directions
At once the skyscrapers break up aluminum
Glass in the vanishing
Point perspective
The childbearing future
Tomorrow, some other day perhaps
I am sitting by the edge of the desk

Your face in analytical terms
The light tailor
Made for her the letter brings in today's no reasoning
Context "I don't love you anymore" is a lie
Paper on which the poet signs his name
"Benedetta"

Immortal Sin

for Marie Cosindas

Work has not shown her methods of the psychological way
Out from her problems. We saw quite clearly into
The open field: We saw the chief
Difficulty; when it appeared, was
The habit of eating too much, was
The habit of allowing her thoughts to
Contradict her emotions.
The feeling of days endlessly long.
Of complete emptiness, was a way
Out of life; the young girl deciding not to move
From one spot in her life to another,
Subjecting herself voluntarily to suffering
To be free from her feelings
Of love for someone to love
Her. A Sunday morning in Cambridge, Mass.
The young girl sits on the floor with her knees bent
And holding her arms; her hands closed over
Mine in the Polaroid photo
The night before lasting forever.

Dante Never Got Over It

Dante never got over it.
He never realized how much idle
Talk was exposed in the streets of Firenze,
How much the dream of the ways
Justified his weakness and strength.
If he could understand what he was
Losing, he would know
How to escape from the miraculous
Without being afraid of losing anything
Because he knows that he has nothing.
Today in New York
I am reminded of the determination
Required of me to understand
The fact that there is no other way.

Long Distance Photo

I was going toward all she left behind
Her. The Italian ethos. She regretted the rain falling.
The stuffed toy clutched in her hand,
To remember herself, briefly;
A child without family
In New York. Her arms around me in the photo
Machine where people never stop kissing.
The radiance of her face,
The composition of the enclosed space,
The unlimited way of looking at ourselves
Six centuries ago in Firenze,
Days of 1966 in Cambridge and New York.
The destruction of emotions.
We are inside the landscape I explained to her.
We have learned to be aristocratic, uncompromising.

*Now this fine body perceives a universe which we do
not ordinarily perceive.*

> —*Aleister Crowley*
> *from* Magick in Theory and Practice

Tomba di Nerone

Now this fine body perceives a universe which we do not
Ordinarily perceive. She cuts across the open
Field to her father's house,
The "most fragile and robust child" of all
Barzini's children; the reconstructions of emotions
Beside the Tomb of Nero
While the sun was bright
That day breaking through the clouds behind her
Head. She could not find her
Dreams come true; soon Benedetta will be interrupted from my life
Story. Her life without emotions.
Nothing would be left of today and of the day
Before. Father and daughter crossing the Via Cassia
Hand in hand.

Her Father

He put his hands upon her head
And disappeared. The Italian
Childhood and the visits to the small church by the sea
At twilight. The emotions missing the expectation of
The young boy to return did not leave
Her mind, her first homecoming, her father
Making olive oil and wine, took her in
His arms: "My most fragile and robust child,"
He said. And going by his words
I held her in my arms;
Sunday morning and the night
Before in Cambridge, Mass. she remembered
Herself; the candlelight circling around
The room forever. The three of us.

Sonnet: Give It a Name

The optimism of remembering oneself;
Tomorrow different from today
And the night before.
Her other self under strobes,
And what's living undergoes
"Change" in sunlight, in candlelight.

She remembered herself bleeding
For the first time
In five years, and for the first time,
Believed in her feelings.
Tomorrow different from tonight and the day
Before: Gerard and Benedetta
Undergoing change in each other's arms.

Her head fit in the curve of my neck in the morning.

Student at Lycée Français de New York

Candlelight in daylight
By the closed window
The diagonal continuity of rain falling
Against the windowpane. A stained glass
Bowl of white roses in focus,
A bowed head in tears. Months later
I walked up to the Lycée Français de New York
At the time of student recess;
The young who are innocent in the universe,
The young who are innocent in love.
But she was nowhere to be found.

Contributor's Notes

I am remembering myself in all places at once:
Cambridge, Mass.; New York City,
Late autumn; "the last few years of her
Struggling and suffering, from within."
Benedetta's hand held
In mine, the open field
Of her vision in the candlelit room,
The Dodge Dart without radio music,
The black hair pulled back in a knot,
Questions and answers
Written on a restaurant menu,
Two faces looking out
From the "4 for a quarter" machine.

An Hour and a Day

She is doing what her grandfather did before
Her, what her father did,
The curiosity which marked her
Coming to New York. The difficulty of
Understanding how not to avoid
What is now the child
Bearing future presented to her
Avoiding what Barzini Sr. saw, covering two
Continents in a motor
Car, hanging from the end of
The chassis when it jumped from the bridge
Somewhere between Kalgan and Kiakhta,
By following the sun across the Gobi Desert.
She is now twenty-three.
Rome on the same latitude as New York,
And what she found there was what he knew
What he saw.

Providence to New York

for Andy

The struggle against the day
Dreams, against sleep,
Passing through the same experiences
In a different order. The bay
Window reflecting the inside
Superimposed on the outside,
The darkness. Andy beside me,
Asleep. Did I understand from what he had said
Once when he picked me up
From the floor out of breath
That knowing enough, we will
Know what to do? I work at my own
Risk to regain what I had
Before, struggling against theories
People impose on my life. Even now
I think differently on the same subject,
On the young girl's life
The chronology of
These poems about her.

Villa Feltrinelli: Porto Santo Stefano

A young girl—
Vineyard and rocks, a distance north of Rome—
Rising thru tall weeds.
Today she can't come to terms with her emotions.
The young girl faces the sea
From the hill at the seaside resort of Tuscany.

She walks to the small church
By the sea.
She stands at the gate of the church.
Maybe she's thinking of not returning to Rome.
But the daydreams and nightmares persist.
At Venice she extended her hand to a hand that didn't exist.

She walks across the open field
Forgetting the diary entry,
Forgetting why she was caught
In the rain falling on her.
The twilight descending, also;
All that is constructive to find her way home.

Cities all over the world where she's been
Taken to and for what
Reason she couldn't be with her father.
The truth that everything happens, happens.
Rome, Montevideo, Geneva, Milano, New York.
Days filled with relative silence.

Identification she didn't want to give
Up, finding herself feeling "dead" inside
Out, deciding to leave
Behind her former life and set home to Rome;
A father to call in the nightsweat.
What circumstances force her away from him, anyway?

Somehow she didn't find

Herself willing to discuss her conscience
Outloud. She preferred her own independence.
Where are the trips to Tuscany and the young girl
Who wound her arms playfully round
The neck of her father in the photo and smiled?

"I am here," he answered, out of
Hearing, out of reach of her own family
History, the literary heritage; her grandfather crossing two
          continents in a motor
Car to find a shortcut to Mantica,
Her father writing non-fiction all over America.

A light falls through
Her hands the wedding dress the gold rings and cross.
Her father said, when she was fourteen,
"You can have it this way."
The daydreams crossing each other.

The weeks continue to sway at her legs
Where she stands in the open field. Tuscany.
Here Giotto came to paint her face
Six centuries ago.
Her father beside her. Her head
In his arms.

Barzini's Daughter

"You should have seen me papa
In my gym class falling to the floor.
I was so graceless, but I am fast learning.
I have to touch things and then draw the line.
I want to go to New York to model enough to study
Acting seriously and everything else, too.
I want to go over the hill today and look around me
At the landscape and the sea.
I want you to come with me papa
If you're not busy."

It's autumn, it's winter.
You look for yourself, the way you looked
As a child, in the "4 for a quarter " photos
Taken today. The light flashing behind your head
Pressed against my left shoulder
And a still-portrait emerges.
The landscape inserted behind us.
The clouds fairly bright in the late afternoon.

Do Not Give Up Your Desire for Children

for Warren Sonbert

In Penn's sensitive photographs
The young girl holds a puppy in the overfold of her
Little brown dress; the paw of another puppy,
Leaping at her
Right side, is preserved in the fold.
The beauty mark noticeable
In every direction the wide angle lens
Seems to contain the sunlight falling on her
What light-leaks are all about:
The result in the sense that you can see more
Rear projection in terms of the past:
Barzini holding Benedetta in his arms.
The short-cut through Columbia campus
1930 subway to Flushing
State Street to 35th Avenue coincide.
The passage of multiple feelings
Through one thought; the trip
Book diary in which secrets are written.
A vicious circle, and so on. Some new
Material I want you to think about.
"Why did I want definitions?" she said.

In the Country a Few Miles Outside of Rome

the long driveway
leads up to the house
in the rain
falling on my head
the grass ignited with sunlight
the young girl's thoughts
in my heart
her father standing behind me
the driveway the garden
the hounds
tooth trousers she wears
as she did on the long drive to Cambridge
the way she looked
when a student at Rome
"delight in minute observations"
the great political landscape of Italy
the family photos the sailboat in full
sail the day's air mail
letters laid out on his desk
losing count of the days
the motor-car increasing its speed in the 60-year dream
rediscovered geographical truths
the young girl, as she passed, smiled at me.

Consciousness Expanding

The current history along the Via Cassia from Rome is
    essentially quiet
And the bleeding sky
Is why I do not
Tell you this—

Can only postpone the final
Result expanding out of
What keeps herself from going
Haywire, from saying her prayers.

The Hotel Navarro is floating on clouds
Of the years 1950–1955
Benedetta Barzini of the underground
Movies, of Dante, of pure personification

Once I looked at a photograph
Her face for so long I became
Half the face I looked at
The consciousness of belief the inevitable encounter

She revealed to me the fate of Giovanna
Laura, Beatrice, Pasternak's Lara
Their lives of all that she no longer would like
To be as she took off her clothes in the candlelit room

A fear to hurt you, to have hurt you.
That is Benedetta talking
Tonight it is the friends I had
Forsaken and her personification in my life too, talking

My contempt for you
You named ignorance and my admiration for you
Servility
When they were among the few things we had
    in common
Your trash and your poses were what I most
    appreciated
Just as you did

And the way you were free
Of me

    —W. S. Merwin
    from "Peasant"
    (A Prayer to the Powers of This World)

Benedetta Barzini

for Rene Ricard

When it is not yet twilight
                    though the Italian girl
out of another life reminds me
                    that I am not dead
in the blue room the candle
light pushed through our dream coming to life
        disappeared into morning

Out of another life
                    her grandfather with Scipione Borghese
coming in the 40 h.p. Itala
                    through the rain and mud
in that transcontinental summer.
                    Unable to find
the place, she is hiding
                    out of contempt
for the young man who loves her.

        The truth that tells

all only once in a life
                    time the way she brings
nothing but her own innocence
to the open field
                    clouds make shadows where she stands.

She comes back to me
                    in another life I am not here
in the collapse of how many
                    years from her death she will live
forever without turning to someone in bed,
turning truth into myth
                    not to see
                              two faces in love
in the black-and-white photo
machine.

She begins to live and die more when she could not
                    explain how not to lie.
The dream taking place—
                    a small private wedding.
the going away
                    and coming back
                              school days
                    the sounds of her class
mates dancing in the gym class
                    with and without her.

Benedetta Barzini   Benedetta Barzini   Benedetta Barzini

how strangely you lean on one leg in the full-color
                    high-fashion spread

still living on nightmares of power and light
leaks. I try to remember your faults,
                    but know the top spinning
secret of looking at you.
                    It is all in
                              how you are living

the universe to which Dante
      attributed your many sins
walking forward and back
      through sunlight rising to paradise
the last faces
    before going under the ice
        return to enter my life.

A director is a man, therefore he has
ideas; he is also an artist, therefore he
has imagination. Whether they are good
or bad, it seems to me that I have an
abundance of stories to tell. And the
things I see, the things that happen to
me, continuously renew the supply.
                    —Michelangelo Antonioni

Snow Emergency Street

All I know is this slow exhibition of greatness.
A description of what's been
Happening. The pain is not
Clearly defined. These are
The eyes of the young girl and that side of her
Character capable of being
Afraid. Across the street young man walks
Back with hands in pockets.
Children's voices at playground
In distance. The sound
Track of tire treads making sharp turns
In the distance.
Water sprinkler being turned off.
A roadway ribbed with white lines where no one is
Crossing. In its beginning was its end.
A woman, a city, an intellect.
The environment of that experience.
After the affirmations
Who will discover the rejections?

"Take Me Home"

My eyesight searches the landscape
for a part of the young girl
I cannot forget: her bourgeois
Sense of everything democratic.
The "4-for-a-quarter" photos extending into our lives.
I despise what theories are
all about "an experiment" she would say
a certain level of life belonging to no one.
I see the clouds above
my head split open
vapor trails of words in the sky.
The bouquet of red roses held against herself.
The open petals falling to the floor
boards about her feet in the night
sweat, the long pause of sunlight.
What she feels she fears
to say, escaping the lies in her
life what lies about her
At Rome on TV. The day
dreams of childhood on fire
to regain contact, fresh air.
This is your bedroom and this is your little stuffed dog
I would say.
I am remembering the young girl in the sunlight all day.

2000

1990

1980

1970

VI. Italian
Photobiography
(previously unpublished)

1960

White Pages

We walk toward the front
row steps of the Duomo at midnight
in handheld eyesight;
fragments of conversation of our fathers' earliest lives
on horseback riding the Great War;
the waterproof watch
tower you were led by the hand to
believe the sea below was not the sexual night
mare recurring inside your closed eyes
seeing and hearing yourself scream
as a child would at age five.
The young girl when she discovered herself growing
thin in a physical state
of not moving in
bed for a month, the LP
repeating itself on the turn
table until the two track sound
system wore itself thin in your ears
and you thought yourself dead
inside or you thought you would die.
The first windy drafts
of long letters you never sent
out from your life
span; the open secret escape
hatch into fresh air and sunlight;
the Milanese underground becoming
a new way out
of moving about
in the profile pose of Franz Liszt.
Why is it my favorite words don't exist
For you? This is a poem about
donna Patrizia on clouds
and these are the earliest lives in the photo
maton. A first national picture.

The First Time I Saw donna Patrizia Ruspoli
Age Six at Forte dei Marme

She stands at the edge of the sea
coming up to her feet,
the face of a child
in the black & white photo.
She's holding a beachball.
Now she's pushing through the weeds
with her hands. She's smiling.
She no longer remembers Marescotti,
her father, in uniform at the charge of command
of a last-minute parachute jump in North Africa.
Now she is a city after the war
assuming consciousness
where life's possible again.
She is its new buildings and its winding muddy river.
She is its favorite new song.
She is its tears.
She is its adolescent hearts in parks on national holiday.
She is its many religious facades and its movie stars.
She is its other stars also.
She's wearing a white jumpsuit.
She's standing at attention. She is an ocean
bather. The wind ruffles
the long, dark brown hair against her
rosy cheek. Now she's more
tall, more beautiful.
The rain lights on her face.
She is this six-year-old child
seeing herself for the first time
in the black & white photo
with surf coming up to her feet.
She is about to tell her life story.

Days of Rome

Days of nothingness
Days of clear skies and temperature descending
Days of no telephone calls or all the wrong ones
Days of complete boredom and nothing
        is happening
Days of 1967 coming to a close in the frigid condition of chest
        cold and cough
        drops
Days of afternoons in the life of a young girl
        not being on time
Days of daydreams exploding
Days of utter frustration
Days of my film being cursed and myself
        with the curse never lifting
Days of closed windows to keep the cold
        out of the livingroom warm
Days of avoiding lunch for a phone-call
        with change of plans for the day
Days of posting letters
Days of no mail today
Days of fatigue and amphetamine highs
Days of Charles Edward Ives
Days of the 4:00 P.M. doldrums
Days of wonder drugs to challenge the common cold
Days of utter frustration
Days of forgetting

Homage To P. Klodic,
painter of ocean liners, ca. 1930s

(upon discovering a poster board print of the S.S Rex.)

In an antique shop
                    on St Mark's Place
I discover you
                    gracefully moving thru a postcard
of waves breaking the sea level surface
around you
                    the lines of your white
boot-topping receding
                    black smoke towering above your two tri
color funnels into blue sky
I only have fragments to go by
the likeness of closing in "distance" (Creeley
observed with one eye
as two) so that I
                    may freely
pass over time & space
                    via nonstop jet
New York–Rome to out-race
you.
         Thirty-five years earlier sailing
the Southern Route, leaning over the railing
Gerardo Malanga could hear the hum
of your engines' swift currents below him
How far did he come
and how long was his journey with you?

                    O my blue
          ribbon prize winner who
made my father's American dreams real
where does your spirit reside
after the fire-bombing on the outskirts of Trieste?
Memories of father beside

me? Where is Captain Francesco Tarabotto who knew
your every vibration by heart?
Waves slowly pulled apart.

You were as beautiful as the idea of you
that first evolved in the minds of the men
                    who designed you
Your rivals named for cities and queens
        were no match for your speed
breaking record
                    the sea levels
off where you cut thru
                            waves synonymous to music
the whitening foam
                    wake at your stern.

For the First Time

for Isabella Albonico

For the first time a young girl smiles
inside the dream
of what I'm seeing
outside myself.
Evening is Rome,
otherwise time disturbs me .

    Isabella you're like a very long evening
and the wishing well of my mind's eye.
    Yet I don't really know you.

Rome is an open city to 1,000,000 stray cats
and time is a turn
table of intimidations and specific events. Sometimes
I feel small
at cold war with the Italian bureaucratic machine,
the paperwork technicalities,
and instead watch for the exact time
and promise of what happens in the sky
light covered by clouds on my way to *Istituto Luce.*

So Rome resembles each of us or
an exposed part of the ancient past in which the present
tense exists. Rome has me
thinking of time and space as a poet.

But time is never enough.
In New York, for example,
I always manage to get things done
having nothing to do with New York.

Further: Time
fails to deliver the mail on time.

Time is a carbon copy.
Time is a Bufferin
commercial.
        Time is hallucinatory.

What shall I tell you of time?
I wonder what time it is in New York?
                  It's winter.
Dropping a name
and address is the pocket
map of Rome I know by
heart.
      Rome is a lot of other things too;
but I can't find time
or the place to tell you,
walking around the city
limits most of the time,
not having your phone number to call.

Sonnet to Edgar Allan Poe

Edgar Allan Poe,
I lived only three blocks from your home
on a street on a hill
a small field once,
beside the little white cottage
I stood in front of your
green-painted gate age four
when my father unconsciously cast
my fate with a little box camera.
I've come this far to Rome
closing in the opposite
distance and my father's 1920 American dream
traveling by steamer via Naples–New York,
not knowing his cause.

The Dawn Patrol

for Elsa Morante

Sometimes I think of Benedetta
or Bice
the permanence of the independent Italian
dead and alive, the father whom she lost
while attending Lycée Français de New York;
the salutary intercession
of Giannalisa's daughter.
Six centuries ago Cilia Caponsacchi
was not aware of Alighieri's poems to her
daughter nor was I aware at my baptism
a young girl was born at a villa outside of Rome.
Today she resides at Milano, sometimes at Rome
at the time when I'm writing
these lines and bowing my head.

A Version of Dino Campana

the room has a red and drooping rosewound
bridge piers make the river more beautiful
arches make the sky more beautiful
arches hold your form silver light more pure on the blue
house more beautiful in the shade of the arches
I observe you all over Italy where the languid step
    lingers in deserted streets
in a moment the roses shed their bloom
the petals fallen because I could not forget the roses
because I could not forget you
on the hillside we search for roses
in another century
this journey
we call love with our trees with our memory
box of the night
sweat before we made roses which shone for a moment
in the morning sun in the warmth of the room
you will turn to dream upon the wan pillow
case I enter your dream as you're dreaming
to breathe the whisper of this slow magnetic dance
your dreams hovering in the sky
line above you
I want to see your hair dance
on your skinny white shoulders
your eye is sparkling
is lovely your eye is perdition
the ivory of your belly surpasses the ivory of the crucifix
I would like to make a fantastic diadem of your tears
and wear it on my head
at the hour of my death to hear the dream
girls speak of me in confidence
the divine simplicity of your clear limbs
how small the world is and the light in your hands

Oggi

Ideas, except that they're sometimes stolen
without attribution
                    as the case today
with my films caught in a deadlock somewhere
at Chiasso.

Don't be afraid of feeling good
inside when everything about to happen happens
as everything must

                    I've discovered
it's more difficult to move about Rome
                    at the 5:00 P.M. rushhour

I walk past Piazza di Spagna to post air-express letters
and go back to where I came
                    from San Silvestro
buy carton of Rothman's, two rolls Tri-X
and *Town & Country* with Marisa Berenson's smiling
cover-girl face.

          Benedetta...   Benedetta Barzini comes up from behind
tugs at my John Keats scarf and I turn around
I am this dead girl's voice
                    and she diminishes for a moment
is it shyness?
          because I'm alive looking at her
only recognition
                    and then loses herself
in the misty twilight

as "a testament to pain's indifference."

Warm Morning 8.18

It's the first anniversary of November 8, 1966.
It's time to get the mail, walk the Lungotevere delle Armi.
It's time to read books, meet Elsa Morante
for lunch.

At the tabacchi a face appears
in the bi-monthly pages of *Vogue*.

On the black-and-white film the same face wavers
and never disappears.

The young boy always remembers you
that way.

In the Republic of Italy he makes an awkward bow.

2000

1990

VII.
Poems
from
the
Seventies
&
Eighties
(previously unpublished)

1970

1960

Cablephoto

for Keith Richards

ROLLING STONES' keith richards
greets girl friend actress anita pallenberg
and their 4-month-old son marlon
on arrival at londons heathrow airport
after u s tour
miss pallenberg a german
said british government has told her
she must marry
or leave England

Today the Inner Voice Speaks of Control

You find yourself in a vacuum at first
there is no turning back
there is nothing identifiable you can grasp
    that you can call your own—
life you can grasp that you can call your own

Instead the body wants to crawl inside the head
It is longing to meet death head on and still shine
It is longing to possess the secret and then letting go
    and still in possession of it
the eyes of the poem go blind

the inner vision takes over
and the mind inside the body sits in one of five empty rooms
the one with the walls that are blank
the one where street noises come crashing through
the room becomes space in which the body remains
still

You can no longer create
your own world,
because your world no longer exists to relate
to

truck noises outside come crashing through
a separate reality comes crashing through
even the inner voice asks *where are you where are you*

The question is *what am I doing here*
the question is *why did I come here*

the question waits to be answered
the body waits to be answered!
the body wants something
but what does the body want
already the body grows weaker

the question is patient
the mind is too busy to even reply
devising ways of escape
devising ways to escape from this city

I begin to lose touch with myself
I begin to not recognize myself
I begin dropping things
I begin losing things
I begin something

I feel the brains spilled out on the sidewalk
the arms flailing
the scream

"Stopping the World" (tentative title)

You become restless
You become restless because you are bored
You become restless because you are bored
                    because your days are empty
and you do not know what to do

How at times you feel ill at ease with yourself:
when you go on trains, or in the streets leading out from the
        Square
you are alone
no one recognizes you
but you want it that way
and you do not know what to do
and you do not know what to say

Little by little, the face of a stranger
looks out from your face at your face
in window reflections. On some days
you stare out into space, acknowledging nothing,
nothing but time passing

Some say, the world you come back to, to live in,
is not the same world, but it's you who have changed
and you realize the difference

You realize why no one can recognize you
because change is the same
because the inner vision takes over
because you're able to see in the dark
because the darkness takes over

Suddenly the road becomes dark
whole worlds become dark
there is only one body

you return home to five empty rooms

you return with eyes tired
limbs numb
arms about to fall off

Here all things begin.
the world you come back to, to live in

all at once energy shows in the eyes
a part of you that survives
a part of you missing

you open your eyes and close them
It is dark. It was always dark.
That's how you came into this world.

You are certain of nothing
but death
but not when,
not where, or how;
not the separate hairs on your head.
but fears within each one

you make yourself new again
you come into existence

but the journey leads you no further,
death can be seen in the distance—
death is a witness:

headlights fixed on the road
that keep coming closer
that keep going further away

you will not exist when I wake
but when you wake
to the world I come back to, live in
the darkness of many worlds closing in

You die even though you live

you will go on remembering the dead
   because you remember yourself

Tell me what you know
you ask yourself

I am in the middle of a poem
and can't answer you now.
I am in the midst of life as it continues.
The poem will answer for both of us.
Cold, wind and sky will answer for both of us.
When everything was snow and thus fear
will answer for both of us.
The poem contains spears
like the pictures on the Shield,
like the vibration of the name you were given at birth

A scream wakes up in a room
a scream that continues long after it cannot be heard
all at once I am back in the body with you
all at once there is only one body
       there is only one voice

I pick up a handful of dirt
and rub my hands with it;

the dream wakes but you are not in it
and I think:

Better to die of fear head on
than to die of a stray bullet

Whoever starts out
toward the unknown
must consent to
venture alone.

André Gide

Bad Days

What is this inwardly power you can't defend yourself from?
What are the symptoms?
You bang into things
you begin slurring your words
        sentences breaking in two
                different places, at times
you begin aching all over
you begin losing your balance

now you will have to be modest

Who will go out from you?
—the nameless will go out from you
    poetry kills you

an angel appeared to that boy
    What appears to you now?
    —fourteen years later

a face appears to you now but the mirror is empty
    is the face of a country of whirlwinds
you step through it

There will be a morning when you can't get out of bed
              when what you relate to will not respond;
                      will no longer respond

There will be a morning,
one morning when you can't prop yourself up
    because the body's harassed, ambushed, roped in,

145

because the body is nearing completion

you want so much to leave a line of breath on the window
you do. You put your hands to the window;
                your face to the window
            the outside superimposed on the face

You see death in the bare trees
you see negative energy—
                a room that is white and containing a hum

        this is where you will come when the body is ready

the window turns white
the table in front of the window turns white

the book on the table in front of the window turns white
        and the table turns white

Now it is morning. A darkness is waking.

Finally you open the window.
You shut your eyes.
A bell in the distance is ringing ...
Time darkens
Time is hell
but still the face is shining inside the window

You want so much to have a body to do whatever you tell it
                    to touch what is wrong
                    to make right what is wrong
                    or to leave it alone

The photos will darken, light darkens
the body slowly turns color

Already a darkness appears around the eyes in the present
already a darkness gets darker
these are the infernal dizzies

already the darkness rejoices!

Now the mail floods in without getting answered
	the mail piles up
	the mail that should be returned to the sender

	or the handwritten drafts that pile up
		without getting typed

You're at the end of one poem and you are beginning another
	or you think you're beginning another
	because the body is swimming inside the head
		the head is drowning

Now you are dreaming of a darkness
now morning wakes
now nothing wakes
you see nothing

Now you conceive your end and run toward it
		you run into the world

The shadow no longer starts at your feet

This poem has given up sleep
	—the poem that's in transit—
	the poem that's for keeps

this poem that continues because it shall have to
this poem that becomes you because it's existing without you

What Happens in Dreams

At night my fears make themselves known in dreams
they shoot out in all directions at once
like a tree that splinters the air with its death
    in several explosions
there is no place to hide in the open
I can see fleeing shirttails in flames!
    in the distance
And that's not all!
I taste my own semen
now my head is under a rock
I want to go deeper
I cling to the rock
    as to my life
The rock is a pillow
I come crashing through
the memory of me on a sled rushing downhill
the same tree that exploded several lines back
    is directly on course
coming closer
I begin writing down what I remember
I fall asleep
suddenly the window enters into the sunrise
suddenly a train comes rushing out of a tunnel
I wake to tell you what happened
the page in the notebook is blank
You get up to go to the bathroom

Autobiography: A Continuum

A poem throughout the years follows me
it waits to be given a title
I give it a title
on p. 54
I give it your name

o

I give it the title of leaves caught by the wind
on Commonwealth Ave
I give it the title of the young girl in the photo
    who clings to the iron wrought fence
        as if it were wholly her own

I give it the title of the train roaring out of a tunnel
                the title of coffee dying slowly in a cup
                the title of the blank page
        upon which a poem is about to be written
            this poem

The Pull of the Vernal Equinox

I reach the clearing but no poem greets me
no poem's in sight
the rest of the poem was never restored
It lies buried beneath the snow
a sled covered with snow

but I've forgotten what I wanted to say
Nothing interesting in the mail today
I dreamt I climbed the ladder leaning against the hay,
but you were nowhere to be found
I begin looking down at the ground
  for a sign, some clue
          that would lead me to you

the buds go on swelling
the crocus bursting out of their shells
the entire crust of the Earth going through its cycle of changes,
tense as the skin becomes tense around the temples and eyes.

Now the cold air seeps through the windows
as if to say, *come forward*
to trick the mind into believing its time

you will come home to find the window wide open
and a wind howling through the rooms of the flat

you close the window
and the scene fades as in a film when it ends

I am watching you closely
a few moments from now even your life would have changed

For the better ... who's to say?
This has all been a dream unable to wake as night becomes day

What rhymes with day?

I am salt strewn on the pavement
I am the shadow that's missing
Something is always missing

There's no comparing how things were and how they are
No way of knowing when this poem began
or if and how it will end
for what there was to make it end

Each night I sleep in a grave
and dream I sleep in a grave
Each night takes all day to end

I dream a long hallway of doors
one by one they open ... they close
"I met him on p. 54"

What am I doing alive? I ask myself waking

Is this what's meant to see for the last time?

The light in the room slowly dims or the optic nerve fades
Which is it?
But the voice in my sleep doesn't answer

I see there's no ending this poem
It goes on for as long as I go on
for as long as I have to,
way past the time when I'm gone
the poem not afraid to go on
on the road that continues without you
in the poem that continues without you

Then you will wake and step into the window
and repeat this poem as if in a trance
there's no second chance
your eyes begin squinting
Suddenly the sun begins shining again
the sun begins shining

You remind me what it is to be human
"I'm making you a sandwich" you say
"I'm writing you a poem" I can hear myself say

I can hear the wind rattling the windows
I can hear the needle scratch across the end of the record

Suddenly I hear my own breathing which the poem carries
        away
We've only somebody's word for it as night becomes day

Conceptual Photographs

Patty Hearst
on bed
cleaning
her gun

o

shopping
in Bergdorf's

o

wearing
crew-neck sweater
and
Villager
skirt

This Is the End of Romance

for Hoé

In the News

Lord and Lady Romsey leaving Romsey Abbey
in Hampshire on Saturday
after their marriage
which was attended by the Queen
and Prince Philip.

Lord Romsey, 32, is grandson
of the late Earl Mountbatten,
and his bride, who is 26,
is the former Miss Penelope Eastwood,
whose father, Major Reginald Eastwood,
founded the Angus Steak House chain.

Daisy Vreeland. She is the 19-year-old
granddaughter of Diana Vreeland, the legend.
A tall blonde with laughing blue eyes
and a rangy figure
who lives in California. She lives
in jeans and sweaters. She's 5 ft 8½ inches
and a dress size of 8

o

BERNSTEIN SPEAKING
You're pretty young, Mr.—(*Remembers the name*)—Mr.
Thompson. A fellow will remember things you wouldn't think
he'd remember. You take me. One day, back in 1896, I was
crossing over to Jersey on a ferry and as we pulled out there was
another ferry pulling in—(*Slowly*)—and on it there was a girl
waiting to get off. A white dress she had on—and she was carry-
ing a white parasol—and I only saw her for one second and she

didn't see me at all—but I'll bet a month hasn't gone by since
that I haven't thought of that girl.

o

You're
there?—

I'll be over
in half an hour

I'll be over
in a minute

I'll see you
soon enough.

o

Brooke Mallory, 11, wears
cranberry tweed blazer
with sailor collar, $70, and
pleated skirt, $40, by
Timothy Dunleavy

o

At Belchertown
a dog chases after a stick
on the town green

Poem Paid with a Dreamed-up N.E.A. Grant

I light a dead match
with a pilot light

for a candle
used for lighting the burner

I let the water boil
for coffee

only to discover
there is no coffee.

Lavorare stanca

footholds
in reality—

not by violence
lost,

though nothing's lost,

  not the rocks silent

  not the high-tension
  wires the
  brown hills, the grey
  apt blocks distant—*Periferie*—

  as witnessed, recorded by
      friend Ugo Mulas, 1954—

  the Milanese twilight

  fields of
  brown grass, rubble,
  bits of plaster,
  red and yellow
  leaves, a deserted shack

  a basin
  to wash
  in, rusted

  children's voices
  empty pockets

but the milkweed or the rain
itself

reaching up
from dirt,

twisted auto fenders

then all is lost to view

where Feltrinelli
met his fate,

blown up

VIII.
Subversion
of the
Pastoral
(previously unpublished)

2000

1990

1980

1970

1960

... gusty
Emotions on wet roads on autumn nights;
All pleasures and all pains, remembering
The bough of summer and the winter branch.

—Wallace Stevens,
from "Sunday Morning"

the body is death

for tad

I'm going to meet death head on
inside a tree
inside myself

I'm going to meet the stars
and one by one name them
name them by heart

I'm walking up a dirt road
and the road is gentle
and beside it a field of barley is singing
and suddenly the light in the sky darkens
and suddenly it's night

I'm going to agree with what I've been in agreement with
for some time
because I'll be given the chance to

I am going to call on the 100 names of one god
I am going to call on the one name of one god
I'm going to seek my ultimate totem
absorb the vibration of Malkuth
I am going to meet death head on
     with its nine constellations of eyes

I am going to meet death head on
     inside a tree split by heat lightning
and it is myself

I'll contact you when I'm able
because I shall have to

We Go Out into the Night

we go out into the night
there is a silence like rain in the glistening leaves
when the bears break out
from sensory instinct into something remembered
into something that darkens
their fur shines in the moonlight
they enter our bodies and are born again
as men crossing our headlights
clothed in bearskin and trying to speak

The Snowy Owl Shudders

I see faces inside me all the same but different
place names dates pushed into dark places
the night lights of the city pushed into dark places
and there are abandoned tracks of a deer
haunted and burning with darkness
The snowy owl shudders.
This is what it's like to hear the sound of a train
with lights turned off
plying its way through a wet field
toward the back of the brain,
but the lights were always turned off
the conductors are sleeping
I start toward the howling with food in my hands
but the train is empty going deeper into these mountains

Leaping Over Gravestones

Because I've had this conversation with the unconscious
I fall asleep screaming
and can almost taste my own semen.
It's mid-June.
The road shining with the rain-reflected lights.
I begin feeling the inside of this body rotting away,
giving way like a weak structure, a light leak.
The dream wakes without me,
like the darkness of a moving train
with no one inside, like darkness inside a car,
this car haunted by the morning it drives through
with its headlights turned on,
haunted by the field it one day will find itself in
with its doors left open and hanging
and its floor rotting through and the wind sweeping through it.
I fall asleep and dream it takes us all winter to climb out
through the ruins of the engine.
I wake and still the energy is inside us:
your hand on the wheel nearing completion.
This is what it must be to feel we're living as we die,
what it must be feeling the ghosts of 75 horses to the senses, stampeding,
with massive shoulders and headstrong and wet and windblown
and giving off light.
A car that has time in it
and a chrome like moonlight the eyes never see.
This is what it's like to be a prayer wheel turning forever.
We want so much to run back up County Road 23
so we can warn the deer of our headlights,
because it would instantly freeze
in that light and forever.
It would be two days before the torn carcass gave itself up to the wind.
I can stand upright again,
walk upright again
inside this dream beginning to wake
with the headlights gone out in the body
and the left hand that covers the eyes
and I almost begin to remember

The Journey

I start for a walk that takes weeks
I meet no one
I hear myself speaking at times in the distance
I sit on a rock
I get up
I begin walking again
I make my way over rocks on a trail
I enter a clearing and in the clearing a house
   with its lights and with no one inside
I enter this house
I recognize the things in this house
   the remembered table
   the remembered chair
I sit at the table
I begin the long journey

The Property

What happened to the frost on the pipes?
the windows of the cottage darken
In another reality children's voices enter and then disappear
For a moment it is morning in late summer
Benno is pulling up weeds
Don waiting for the water to boil for a cup of coffee to start the day
Irene walks across the lawn to the Stone House or she doesn't
an occasional car pulls up the driveway

the scene changes
there is snow on the ground almost blue in the moonlight
the end of the driveway touches darkness
the kitchen is an absence
What happened to the children's voices
What happened that I should see the changes
I think I become invisible
I am mistaken. I am correct.

Remembering the Berkshires

I think of the third day snow had fallen
it was still falling at night when I returned

the snowbound tracks and bridges are a dream
the embankment is black
the log of a fir tree uprooted

though only one year has gone by
a stream has emerged from the thicket at night

in a house on a mountain someone is turning out the light
someone is going to sleep at last

now the moon is in capricorn
shadows fade toward morning
the days move on like a diary
everything is still
the same but something is different
and it is myself

and the pressure of the wind increases

Eban

I come back an afternoon walking through fallen
leaves bunched together with mud, realizing my life
is no longer in touch with the depth of the naming
of things. I look around me. Not even the books
in my library are helpful. The shelves sag, the
dust collects. Eban runs up to me; his body is black
and shiny like the descriptions of forests in fables
I remember reading beside the warm fire, and I think of
wool that has taken on the odors of woodburning stoves
in winter. He has been silent for thousands of years.
There is something I want to say to him ... I am like
you. The silence in you has entered into my own body.
Perhaps you will tell me something.

IX. Robert Moses 1888–1981, Coordinator of "Limited Objectives"
(previously unpublished)

2000

1990

1980

1970

1960

Robert Moses 1888-1981
Coordinator of "Limited Objectives"

HE IS A MAN OF FEELING.
HE IS SIX FEET PLUS.
HE HAS THE TORSO OF A HORSEMAN,
THE BROAD SHOULDERS OF A TRAINED SWIMMER,
THE SLIM LEGS OF A RUNNER,
HIS STRONG BUT SENSITIVE HANDS WITH TAPERING FINGERS,
SELDOM AT REST, SUGGEST THOSE OF A SCULPTOR.
HE IS FIRM-JAWED, AND HAS HEAVY, DARK EYEBROWS.
WHEN HE IS IMPATIENT OR AROUSED,
HIS RATHER SMALL AND SOMBER DARK BROWN EYES
CONTRACT AND FOCUS ON HIS STRAIGHT, EXECUTIVE NOSE.
WHEN IN A FIGHTING MOOD HIS JAWS SNAP,
HIS CHEEKS AND LIPS TURN WHITE, AND THE
BLOOD SEEMS TO LEAVE HIS FACE.
WHEN HE CALMS DOWN
   COLOR RETURNS TO HIS SMOOTH,
   OLIVE-HUED SKIN, AS HE BREAKS
   INTO BROAD GRIN OR INFECTIOUS LAUGHTER.
HE HAS A LARGE, GENEROUS, GOOD-NATURED MOUTH
   AND STRONG, GLEAMING WHITE TEETH.
HIS SMILE IS DISARMING AND WINNING.
HIS FROWN IS FORMIDABLE.
HIS IS NOT A MIDDLE-OF-THE-ROAD TEMPERAMENT.
HE DOES NOT USE TOBACCO OF ANY KIND.
HE EATS ALMOST ANYTHING BUT RED MEAT,
AND LIKES A SOCIAL DRINK BUT PREFERS SCOTCH. NO MIXED DRINKS.

HE IS NEVER INDIFFERENT, APATHETIC, OR NEUTRAL.
HE IS EITHER FOR OR AGAINST BUT NEVER EITHER/OR.
HE LIKES TO PLEASE AND NOT BE DISPLEASED.
HE FIRST REACTION TO BAD NEWS IS APT TO SHOCK THE BEARER.
NEXT TO BAD NEWS, HE IS INTOLERANT OF STUPIDITY,
   STUFFINESS, IGNORANCE AND TIME-WASTING.
HE APPRECIATES THE COMPLIMENT OF BEING TOLD A THING *ONCE*.

HIS OFFICES ARE PLEASANT AND MODERN,
WITHOUT BEING ULTRA MODERN.
THE WALLS COVERED WITH ATTRACTIVE PICTURES OF PARKS,
SCENICS, BRIDGES AND OTHER COMPLETED PROJECTS.
BUT THE LARGE PRIVATE OFFICE IS DOMINATED, NOT BY REMINDERS OF
PAST ACHIEVEMENTS, BUT BY FACILITIES FOR PROGRESSING
WORK UNDER WAY AND AS AIDS TO FUTURE PLANNING.

HE USUALLY EATS LUNCH IN THE OFFICE WHERE HE HAPPENS TO BE
WORKING—LIGHT LUNCHES, CONSISTING LARGELY OF SANDWICHES.
A FLOOR PACER, HE IS ALWAYS JUMPING FROM HIS CHAIR
AS THOUGH UNABLE TO ENTERTAIN AN IDEA WHILE SEATED.
WHEN TALKING, HIS FACE PROVIDES A KIND OF EMPHASIS.
WHEN HE LISTENS, HE MAY SIT FOR A MOMENT ON, BUT NOT AT, A DESK
     OR TABLE.

HIS MAIL IS HEAVY, BUT TAKING CARE OF IT
IS THE LEAST IRKSOME OF HIS MANY CHORES.
A LETTER USUALLY BRINGS AN INSTANT REPLY
BY RETURN MAIL, IF IT IS NOT ANSWERED BY TELEPHONE.

HE DOESN'T LET WORK PILE UP AND IS ABLE
TO CONSERVE HIS OWN ENERGY AND TIME.
HE DOES NOT LOOK OR ACT LIKE A BUSY MAN.
HE ALWAYS HAS TIME FOR THE AMENITIES, WILL
STOP IN THE MIDDLE OF A SERIOUS DISCUSSION
TO TELL, OR LISTEN TO, AN AMUSING STORY OR JOKE.

HE ADMITS HE DOESN'T READ AS MUCH
AS HE SHOULD, AND DEPENDS ON MRS. MOSES
AND HIS DAUGHTERS TO SELECT MOST OF
HIS CURRENT READING, BOTH AS TO BOOKS AND MAGAZINES.
AS FOR LITERATURE HIS TASTES HAVE CHANGED
LITTLE SINCE HIS DAYS AT YALE AND OXFORD WHEN HE REVELED
IN EIGHTEENTH-CENTURY WORKS.

HE HAS NEVER CARED MUCH FOR THEATER,
PROBABLY FINDING ENOUGH DRAMA IN REAL LIFE.
MOVIES DO NOT APPEAL TO HIM—AT LEAST

HE WILL NOT TROUBLE TO VISIT THEM.
HE GETS MUCH THE SAME KIND OF DIVERSION FROM RADIO
AND TELEVISION.
HE ESCHEWS CROSSWORD PUZZLES, TRIES HIS HAND AT
DOUBLE-CROSTICS OCCASIONALLY,
BUT IS BETTER AT GIN RUMMY.

HE NEVER CARRIES MONEY AROUND WITH HIM
AND FREQUENTLY HAS TO BORROW SMALL SUMS
FROM HIS CHAUFFEUR OR FRIENDS TO MEET EMERGENCIES.
WHEN HE AND HIS WIFE DINE IN RESTAURANTS
SHE SLIPS HIM THE MONEY UNDER THE TABLE TO PAY THE CHECK.

HE IS EQUALLY INDIFFERENT TO CLOTHES.
HE LOVES TO WEAR OLD SUITS, ESPECIALLY FLIMSY SEERSUCKERS.
HE IS, IN MOST INSTANCES, THE MOST INFORMALLY ATTIRED
AT PUBLIC FUNCTIONS. HE LOVES TO WEAR HATS.

HE ATTENDS FEW OFFICIAL FUNCTIONS
OTHER THAN THOSE
IN WHICH HE IS DIRECTLY CONCERNED, SUCH AS
THE OPENING OF A BRIDGE OR PARKWAY,
OR WHERE HE HAS, FOR SPECIAL REASONS, AGREED TO SPEAK.
HE INSISTS THAT HIS WORK, NOT HIS PERSONALITY, IS WHAT MATTERS.
HE IS MOST SUCCESSFUL IN PROMOTING PUBLICITY
REGARDING HIS PUBLIC ACTIVITIES.

HE LIMITS HIMSELF TO OCCASIONS GIVING HIM
OPPORTUNITY TO SPEAK
ON PHASES OF HIS WORK,
TO EXPOUND HIS PHILOSOPHY OF GOVERNMENT,
HIS IDEAS OF PUBLIC ADMINISTRATION,
OR TO GIVE HELPFUL ADVICE TO UNDERGRADUATES.

HE DOES HIS WORK WITH WORDS.
HE'S A FAR GREATER WRITER THAN SPEAKER,
AND HIS SPEECHES READ BETTER THAN THEY SOUND.
HE IS AT BEST AS A DEBATER—
NOT IN A SET DEBATE, BUT IN SUCH ROUGH-AND-TUMBLE ARGUMENTS
AS OCCASIONALLY TAKE PLACE BEFORE THE BOARD OF ESTIMATE

OR THE CITY COUNCIL.

HIS DOES NOT MANAGE HIS OWN FINANCES EFFICIENTLY
AND HAS, IN THE PAST, BEEN EXTREMELY NEGLIGENT
IN HANDLING HIS OWN INHERITANCE.
HE DOES CONSIDERABLE WRITING AT HOME,
AND TAKES ON SPECIAL CONSULTING JOBS
ON HIS OWN TIME, TO PIECE OUT
THE FAMILY INCOME.
HE IS NOT RICH, AND HIS PUBLIC SERVICES
HAVE MEANT SACRIFICES BY HIM AND HIS FAMILY.

HIS PUBLIC AND PRIVATE LIFE ARE DELIBERATELY
AND PURPOSIVELY KEPT ENTIRELY SEPARATE.
WHEN HE IS OFF DUTY, WHEN DIVESTED OF OFFICIAL STATUS,
HIS OBJECTIVES ARE LIMITED TO PRIVATE CONCERNS.

HE AND HIS WIFE LIVE A MORE OR LESS FORMAL LIFE IN NEW YORK,
ENTERTAINING AT HOME OR ATTENDING DINNER PARTIES.
HE IS ESPECIALLY FOND OF PARTIES
AND ALWAYS HAS A GOOD TIME.
HE IS NATURALLY SOCIAL AND LIKES PEOPLE.

DURING SUMMERS HE HAS A FULL FAMILY LIFE.
HE SEES MORE OF HIS GRANDCHILDREN
AND GETS MORE RELAXATION
WHEN THEY OCCUPY THEIR PLACE IN BABYLON
    AND LIVE A SMALL-TOWN LIFE.

FISHING IS A GREAT SOURCE OF PLEASURE FOR HIM.
HE IS A MAN OF FEELING.
ON SUMMER NIGHTS HE GOES DOWN TO A DESERTED BEACH ALONE
AND SWIMS FAR OUT TO SEA.

X. Three Diamonds

2000

1990

1980

1970

1960

Joan Miró and His Daughter Dolores

I wanted
        always
      to transfigure us
      into
            the painting by Balthus
of Joan Miró
         and his daughter Dolores leaning into him

with your right hand placed over his wrist
and left hand pressed on his knee
for support. His left hand coming in from under
and across the chest
           gently

and both looking directly into the camera.

I wanted always to begin with that—

to begin with
  the
attitudinal
stance
     of
arms drawn behind
arched back,
        windswept hair.

I want to instill the subject with a sense
of self recognition
and to honor what the eye sees.

Eban wants to be in the picture.
He curls up against your knee
for attention
          and I take the picture
before placing myself in the

picture with you,
before the sun swings behind the bldg
across the street
and we lose the light for the better part
of the day

and

3:ii:81 n y c—*The Naked Aura*

Aura, 11-yr-old Eurasian :—you are not eleven

you are precocious   you are an atmosphere

       you are an urbanite

and this is not the first poem
written for you—
         a poem
by Hubert Havlick
predates

is basically irrelevant—so begins the legacy
of wch what I say now is but a continuation
            and perhaps not as friendly

but if we meet in the street
six years hence

        wch brings me
        to my own sense
        of THE DISTANCE
        to be covered
        in time and space
        and as such
        of what options exist—
              passing glance defining
              brink of accessibility

             speculation of
               what we might do

             something fated,
            hopeless even

       where the emotions run wild,

where the afterglow lingers

what will you know
what will
                you remember

1 9 8 7 :

I will be a friend
to your friend, who will
say "Aura, this is Gerard, Gerard ... Aura,"

as if the past didn't exist
in those terms:

        summer dresses
        out on line
        to dry

        the
        spring
        rain

        the flat
        chest filling out slowly

        the aperture,
        the labia minora,
        downward, outward and backward
        for about an inch and a half
            nearly absent now

        and the underarms
        washed once a day

        the nipple dark
        the deep dark eyes

to live long or to live quickly

to be psychoanalyzed

you will be shirtless, long-legged, possess a bitch
attitude—

sweat a little

as if it were all happening long ago
and inside a book depicting
pre-Renaissance times

you will be facetious
you will be promiscuous, spiritless

save in the coming together

… a finger until an inch or so in …

seized by a foolishly contrived fantasy,
a history of futures

of all that is possible but cannot be

no use yr playing *innocent* with me

pleasure, Socrates sd, is to be attained
only thru moderation—

to have not known you
is to've known you

so I'll stop right here.

You may forget but

Let me tell you
this: someone in
some future time
will think of us

                    —Sappho, #60*

The Gift

                    for Simone Federman

dark-
complexioned, mouth pale, hair wet with rain
        reflected light
                small-breasted under black cashmere

or black Lycra maillot   feet

                hands

                wrists

                & teeth showing, that profound
                    angle of nose, look of
                    intelligence, fleeting

                expressions of human face
                            cheerful

                            not too
                            cheerful

                            depending... (have I
                                sd it all?

---

*Sappho, #60, translated by Mary Barnard.

TO HONOR WHAT THE NAKED EYE SEES
in you is a crisis.

Each poem is an act of crisis.

All forms are dead except one.   I probably
                            wldve
                    never read
                    SAPPHO
                        had it not

                            been
                            for you
                    and I've
                    yet to
                    engage
                    you
                    one on one,

                    so this
                    poem will

                    have to do,
                    as appropriation
                    as such,
                        vicarious

                    in ways
                        getting close
                    without being noticed.

                            Touch
                            and go all
                            the way

                    Or the lust
                    in the heart
                    is only pure insofar
                            as

a consummation
is reached.

The notion that
style—such as
that quality
you seemingly possess—
is not surface attribute,
but more of an inward clarity you might

not be even remotely aware of in yourself. No matter.

The Nature of the Beast in me is to that extent
curious inasmuch
as you are as object to your own sex and juices, function
as such:

admire it from afar but don't get your hope up, right?
[is not a question

Do I even have permission
needed
to enter this poem

to join you?   [is not a question

How can I be more convincing?   [is not a question.

There is no pre-dawn light
no bird-noises or street noises, no rosebud, emptiness even
no early roosters
nor sound of tossing and turning unconscious
not the rain
on blank windowpanes wch I miss

nor sound of the clock.

Nothing to rearrange finally.

It will be morning where I surface
with blue-green eyes
and Heaven is an Olympic-size swimming-pool HIGHBRIDGE
     500 feet above sea-level
       giving the illusion
         of being level with soundless
               fast-moving clouds.

     And as the sight of you—the slope of
           back and
              shoulders—pulling yourself up
            from the tiles, the head,
              the soft underarm hairs
                dripping wet,
             and catching the light
                  back-lit

           I become only
            half a self
              momentarily.

Take a toke off a joint.

Nothing, nothing remembered really.

Sit back.   Relax.
Dream again.   Think it all thru.

Rehearse lines, dates, places. Countdown. Everything going great!
           Timing it just so
         that no choice exists
        or suddenly
          it all backfires.

               Back to the
               drawing board!

               Regret nuthin
               though that's a lie.

Regret only what was not
finished, regret only
the loss of the
            other's
            option,

        of what was
otherwise imagined—

    projected, that is:
the cold sudden rain
of 6:30 a.m.
        enters
        the
        unconscious,

    the smell
of your hair
what
    else?

    the small
of your
back?

Who sd what, when is irrelevant. It's tellin the story.
                It's all
movement. It's all nonexistent. Fortunate enough
to share a brief moment
exchanging identities, albeit ambiguities, with you.
                But not now.

We'll have reason to
remember each other   but not now.

Unlike their subjects no two poems are ever the same
nor each having the
power
        to create the desired/decisive

situation
        whereby
you'll respond,
                become
                    real,
            for one lifetime
                    only

                    as in a
                    fashion
            photograph:

            the hair
            is
            windblown

            … evenly made up   [talkin to myself again

Is the person
worth the
                inspiration?   Am I
                        worth the time
                        it takes

                        to absorb
                                it
                                all,

                    throw it
                        all
                            out?

and who's transformed?

o

o

Is this dream of the future any different
than say, to anyone or me, the dream of April
12th come true finally—Fanelli's Bar, corner of
                          Mercer & Prince
                                        where it's
                                        lunchtime
                                        Saturday.

Shall I send you the dry-cleaning bill?
          Shall I send you a mixture of flowers,
          a book of poems, *this* poem,
                              shake hands?

          There are too few things eternal
                              wch is why I take
          final
          pleasure in you. Wch is why there is always something to
          touch or feel or smell or see
          sleeping on one arm face down, and
                                        partially uncovered.

          You are now two people simultaneously: the one
          whose life exists outside this poem
                              and the one entirely made up.

          How prevent the poem from ending now.

Art Project : Mystery Woman, Ongoing Sighting

Hart ... Hart Crane [age 17], when he first came
to New York from Cleveland 1916, lived
in a rooming house at 139 East 15th Street,
within one block of where you live now.
The bldg no longer exists.

This poem is meant to honor what the eye sees
at any given moment—to restore desire to the eye—
such as seeing you in sleeve-
less shirt and shorts. Armpits moist.

"Anatomy is destiny" —Freud.   Bitch-goddess.

This poem is the desire to enter the life
of the person I've already photographed.   [bla bla
This poem is the photo
of the "Girl in Fulton Street" by Walker Evans, 1929.

This poem is using available
light when taking the picture.
This poem is justifiable aesthetic.   [bla bla

This poem is how sexuality appears
in relation
to my own separation
from any real
contact with you
like, for instance,
what I look at profoundly affects what I do,
so I follow you,
for 11 (eleven) blocks in the pouring rain:
15th to 10th along Third   [5 blocks
10th west to Bway   [2 blocks
South on Bway to Waverly Pl   [3 blocks
West on Waverly
to the corner coffee shop at Mercer   [1 block
where I let go of the scent,
or rather it was raining
and I wasn't about to stand out
in the rain waiting for you
to re-appear (because I've better things to do
                    like finally realizing this poem

after several months of seeing you and not seeing you.   [bla bla

I could just as soon be living a lie
Where everything is made up, including your name   [wch I don't know
                                    address   [wch I know

personal history, biographical data.
I could say the shill-picture I made of you
    just at summer's end ['82]
                            was of someone else.

I could say none of this really happened
I could say Hart Crane was fiction also.

"Who art thou, then?"
"Part of the Power which eternally wills evil
and eternally works good."

—Goethe, Faust

Title:
Poem for William Carlos Williams
who wld have written a poem for Sarah Walker
had he been alive to see her now:

to the girl in the red-string bikini,
East Bath House, Jones Beach—
the odds of seeing her again: unlikely

to Meg   of Down to Earth, Seventh Avenue South

to Vicki, Cornelia St. Cafe

to that mystery woman of no. 9 Charles St—

    on the street every day, or every other day
    walking with limp, ice cream
    cone in hand
    or coming out of the Homer, 11;30 A.M.
    or midnight thereabouts / Hopper's "Nighthawks" light —

lives also in a world apart

fragments:

faces
never to
be seen again

as possibility

to WilliamCarlosWillams, his memory

who knew
to make
full use of
possibility
    about such things: "… flat-bellied
                                     in worn slacks upon the street
                                     where I saw her.

street-corner
or subway
sightings   o

                           Her
instances   hips were narrow, her
                                   legs
chance of   thin and straight. She stopped
eyes even

                     me in my tracks— until I saw
so-called   her
passing glance: disappear in the crowd." (end-quote

the eye restless

        to pass beyond
        the moment of meeting…

        to seize the moment—

        or to be lost in the anticipation

Or, likewise, "Distance
is the soul of the
beautiful" says Simone Weil.

Or today, to Archie Ammons of Ithaca
New York, snowbound, shoveling out driveway;
by window-light, writes: *Can I have that virgin?*

        nope:

why?

she's taken:

who says?

'ciety.

to Sarah Walker—the word is *loveliness,*

not entirely inaccurate, and not
being used to such talk—she says:

"Your poems are intimidating."

                       an intolerable language
                    that will frighten—

D. H. Lawrence

Henry Miller

William
Carlos
Williams

to Villon who praised folly and appeared solid
                and paid the price for it

to The Company of Men (poem by Olson of same
title)—Phil ringing me up with
news of latest conquest
or downfall, as it were,
vicarious, carnivorous, i.e.,   "I followed
                    her legs for
                    3 blocks

because that's
what was
walking"—

the obsession

to follow

to wonder

or Paul:

  northeastern shore
Shell Beach, Shelter Island

gale warnings
up along the coast, stating

Yesterday is dead
by the way
what-is-to-be departs from
what-has-been

to compare notes
the day's events
the hipster's walk

the stud's tour
of New York City
                    via 10-speed

a warrant is out for the arrest of all three

for making full use of possibility,   for

having conspired
to invent a world,
as indeed it is—

a threat to the peace
and harmony of so-called traditions, or:

discovery
is praise

>*to the teeth, to the very eyes*

not meant
to be
"intimidating"

or
the will to
love those
who cannot love—

>that's trouble!

Rather observe
the time of day in wch things occur, the air's
clear coolness—Sept. 3rd
to be exact—and Acey Stasip,

from across West Broadway—corner of Spring—
rather than meet head-on, turns abruptly,

eyes averted in fear,

walks south to avoid encounter,

>to avoid
>the self

>to be always
>as thought
>grown old—

to be always in the distance,
against the excrement of some sky
with the turning of leaves

whose partial history—
a self inflicted emptiness

This is the History of Romance
and this is the series of photographs,
each torn in half

      o

(Who is it that said:
Have I imagined
beauty
where there's
none, where none exists   —even now

What use is beauty
unless it affirm a truthfulness / the cliché

Is poetry to be trusted?

Am I to be trusted!

(What difference does
it make?) that I
make a fool of myself, mourning the lack
of grace, or courage wch, in fact,
she dares not acknowledge—

              all manner of association
              become libelous

And for that
        the beauty is
                lacking,
the words are
lacking
            beauty has been
            made cheap,

        in this instance)

                        o

                    She stood
                    to undress in the semi-dark, the lights
                                                    off,
                    awkwardly silent

                    the face half turns away,

                    pulling down panties
                                    slowly
                    the small firm breasts
                    pulled up

                            by the arms
                                    outstretched

                            sliding shirt off
                            overhand

                    the pudendum
                            covered by the
                                        hands

                    the lean belly.

                    the right leg raised,

                    the other leg

                    stretched out
                                    also bare

            the head tilted back

            the underarms, the
                inner thigh
                                    moist

                                            —Cut/

—to the long body stretched
out negligently on the dirty sheet
flat on her back, on a mattress
on the flr of the attic
                    East Hampton
                                    though sleepless

                                    sleeps,

                                    the head pillowed

                                    the soft breathing

        to the labia majora, to the
        convolutions of the orchid
        with rain on it,

        to the grass with rain on it

        and the rocks
        wch are to be

        found
        everywhere

        to "Heatspell, 1938, Children Sleeping
        on the Fire Escape, the Lower East Side"

by Weegee (10 x 12½)

to the Redwing Blackbird, a
North American bird—of the species *Icteridae*
or in Europe *Agelaius phoeniceus*
the male of wch
has scarlet patches
on the wings—an Old World

       songbird, European Thrush.

      o

Ingrid Koolhoven / Natalie Geary

      o

East Hampton (June) 1980: She looks to the sea and,
                           restless, walks to the water's edge—
                           maillot pulled tight into the
                           crotch—stands momentarily, haughty,
                           legs apart, one hand to chin, presumably
                           the other dropped to the side,

                           the delicate wrists

                           the hair loose at the temples,

                           tilting hips,

                           looking out

                           the surrounding sky

                           the dark outline
                           of the shore,

sits with legs crossed
now, half in
the water

       —fade out/

the overall picture is summer

It is a scene from Cape Cod
transported

to eastern Long Island

And the mind is stirred by this scene, the shining waters

—the long body, the back of it,
against a backdrop the pattern of waves:
white foam/royal blue sky,
as the wind whistles—and the small birds
will bring seeds, make a nuisance of themselves

crumpled up newspaper
    rolls across the sand

              the storm
          bursts and fades

gulls screaming,
children-voices far down the beach
playing ball, laughing, calling to each other—

the humility of it all

it is a classic picture

to Dr. Williams—if he could've been alive for this!

to the sound of waves

to a cat injured in the road
and rubbing head with paw
a ways from the beach

to have met people you
can at least talk to
to the sweetsmelling primrose
                growing close to the ground/poised, now open

and to the rainwater that lies there, too

to the rain itself
should there be none or very little
to really matter

or, elsewise,
driven against some breaker
jutting out into a sea

to the belief in the power of beauty to right all wrongs

                as one watches a storm
                come in over the water

to the first light of day, Mulberry St

to a life, a life in wch the poem
of her existence attests to it

to Sarah Walker (I write this
thinking of you), innocent in that light

                        knees hugged tight

                        up into chest

small patch of
pubic hair

revealed
in natural light

It's close to 8:30 A.M.

sunlight thru clutter of venetian blinds

the sounds of rooster
and hen

from poultry mart up the street. Imagine!

piano lessons across the way—Chopin, a part of "The Preludes."

Breakfast
consisting of

coffee, toast,
and jam

yesterday the heat was oppressive

Now Summer, now Fall begins.

Beyond the first words of the poem there is nothing
to know about you.

XI. Mythologies of the Heart
(published 1996)

2000

1990

1980

1970

1960

Andrea Bankoff
from a letter postmarked December 4, 1963
—Beverly Hills

I was supposed to write
but didn't.

As always one is distracted.

Yet some sense

specific

to who you are

remains:

night spent in your parents' attic

the warm flesh
beside me

the bare mattress

the bits and pieces
of conversation,

the contact-sheet of you
naked, the firm breasts

Wordsworth's "recollection

in tranquility,"

the key to finding you—

nothing to go on now.

Underground Woman

Asleep at last:

Jung's four functions—

thinking

feeling

sensation

intuition

"The Art of Observable Dreams"

Days, weeks, months
sometimes years

　　　　o

Having come this far

"Underground Woman"

　　by

　Kay Boyle

Faith... Faith Franckenstein,

her daughter;

only child
by that marriage.

Where had she been
inside my psyche?

Letters

photographs

that useful
sense of past.

Wordsworth's "recollection
in tranquility" come true:

Borough of Richmond—1962

black pebble beach, South Beach

the Narrows

fucked

afraid to come
at first,

but did, finally.

Swam in total darkness. Opaque night

No swimsuit

no moonlight

no one else

no afterthoughts,
but now

circumstance of time

sitting cold wind back

Dried off
on towels

stolen
from
dorm

nearby college

top of
Grymes
Hill

Later,
back somehow
to winding road,

Bay Street

Chill in air now

edge of
woods
asleep.

Whereabouts Unknown

Anne van der Hoof. Met at the 2nd annual NY Bookfair.
Niece of a former governor of Colorado. We raptured each other
standing up on the Esplanade under the parklight in Bklyn Hts.
Said she'd write. She never did. (Who would?!) Moved.
Left no forwarding address.

Lize Thulin, student at Simon's Rock. Parents living in
Paris. Brief encounter, Melvin's Drugstore, Gt. Barrington,
June, 1973.

Deirdre LaPorte, one-time member of rock group known as
Stoneground; went off to New Mexico. A couple of notes.
Then nothing.

Carolyn DeBenden, fashion model. Never spoke to each other,
though she was girlfriend of a friend. Burnt out in New York.
Returned to Paris.

Janet, niece of poet Bill Hunt's wife, Marjorie, Chicago,
June 1973. Long shiny black hair and brackets on teeth.
Left note on bed which read:

> "I would like to touch your hand,
> your face and talk of gentle things—
> now I am alone."

Susan Quick, b. March 20, 1943, my birth-date, chance meeting
Alice's Thanksgiving feast, Stockbridge School, 1971.

Bobbi Shaw, Max's Kansas City, Fall 1966.
Wrote me my first fan letter. On her way to Hollywood.

Andrea Bankoff, Sept. 1963. Party on the Santa Monica Pier.
Went back to motel room. Andy trying to break thru chain
on door while in bed. He's pissed. Dress quickly. Went to
her parent's home in LA. Up all night in attic. Morning.

Catch bus back to Santa Monica. Half-asleep on beach
while Andy reads reviews of Elvis paintings outloud to himself.
Three years later we return to LA. A different scene entirely.
Went to visit. No name on door. Found no one home.

Carol Chalik, teenage romance, circa 1960 Bklyn, staring out
in photo-machine forever.

In the Kaaterskill

There's a scene where Dr. Yurii Zhivago
is seated at writing desk
and branches are rattling the windowpanes
and gusts of snow
blowing every which way
in the yard.

There's a close-up
words linked
on the white paper

Lara is asleep in one of the upstairs rooms.
The Urals blanketed in white.

You would think all this
was more than enough for a poem.

But wait. It's Spring now
in the Kaaterskill
and all this is happening
somewhere else.

You will hear, coming from within, a voice
that leads to your destiny. It is the voice of
desire, and not that of any desirable being.
                                    —Georges Bataille

The Little Schoharie

The route of
the M.& S. Railroad
coming from within ...

for miles in a north-south direction
nothing
but broken-up ties, a faint echo.

So ... coming down from Vromans, Davis Crossing,

I've got to believe you don't exist.

You don't mind, do ya?

The hum of an insect,
the tremor of uncut grass.
Kitchen table. The mountain covered in mist.
The purples and grey-greens of flowers.

CUT: Night falls. The moon disappears.
You represent more the im(age) of beauty
in erotic terms: You appear
open-minded, dreamlike, deserving
of a poem. How presumptuous of me.
Not everyone wants to be written about,
no matter how sincere
the intention. What makes this any different
from let's say how Courbet's *Le Sommeil* (1866)
is viewed, or the violence of an embrace, known as *rapture*
seduction and passion.

I take nothing for granted.
I take my mind off the mundane.

I try visualizing what your paintings might be
the moment before stepping into the studio,
all light and air, the smell of turp,
an oak floor, a low armchair,
cat purring
unsized canvas rolled up in one corner,
military jetstream on distant horizon,
a slight rain, then no rain,
an open field sloping out back into a lap,
the dusty yard, chickens, or was that
the eternal part of the dream where suddenly
you're no longer "separate,"
as in "separate realities,"
but submerged
into
the four o'clock light.
Speck of paint on brow. Perspiration
wiped clean. Blue Navy workshirt
unbuttoned, catching the light.
What am I getting at, you wonder.

Simply that the eyes are
what the soul sees through,
or some such thing,
if I remember correctly
Ezra Pound's remark
is another way stating
Are you as smart as you look, or are looks deceiving?
like the bones in a face. Hence my gaze
is fixed. Hence the wind from the south side
is writing these lines.
The Schoharie below is a mirror
on the wall opposite. Your eyes close
the book in your lap.
The sky empties.

   I'd rather deny this poem
's existence, so that the desire would cease,
so that the erotic moment would cease.

Memorial Day

Two used condoms
almost saffron in color,
get trashed finally—

forgotten I'd put them
in desk drawer—a window

now looking out at East Mountain,
a hill really,
when suddenly I look inward:

the weekend before
hands clasping breasts
from behind full moon
out same window

My young Siamese, Archie
licks his black balls, anus, rolls
over in framed sunlight
reflected on floor,
goes cross-eyed,

meditates.

How They Didn't Meet

She never responded to his pkg the 11th Apr '92—

the Gagosian catalogue, Jasper Johns's "According
to What," which dates from 1964—
                                        and so
she never sent
the postcard, thanking him
with her
phone number on the 15th,

so there was no way he cdve called then
to set up the rendezvous—the meeting itself—
the night of May 2nd Woodstock

and it hadn't rained as predicted
that night after all, a backroad
to Schoharie County
likewise instant rapport
because
next day he headed
north to Barrington
by way of connecting bus
thru Albany
and then on to Pittsfield ... the window
reflecting
            the inside out
on his face in the movable light ...
and the light begins to fade,

so none of what they'd
experienced or the morning after
had ever occurred

—not the Beaujolais '88
not the thraldom
not the bath the soapy insides,
Turkish towels the head
birdlike catching the light
not the kissing of feet ...

not the scent flesh on flesh makes ...

and there is no wind shhhhhhh in the spruce out back

no sun hiding in tree behind cloud

and that ... and that his letter 4 May
and her hand-painted card, also 4 May
never crossed in the post ...

that much is certain,

or her letter May 7th,
inadvertently dated April,
and the phone-call wch followed are hearsay

and the night of the full moon
the 16th is hearsay ...

all is hearsay

virtually no reference
among his papers
that would lead one
to surmise
it had been otherwise

nothing to link them

... and Beatrice Portinari
is not all in pure white,
between two older ladies,

—is not crossing the Ponte Vecchio, ca. 1283,
wch wdve made her eighteen,

but a figment of Alighieri's imaginings,

or had she passed thru—the wildflower
scent in her hair—
it wdve been at a time
he was elsewhere in Florence

and so
would not have known
how she appeared or what was not said
in the language of eyes meeting eyes

take back what is lost
give back what is gained

or Nora ... Nora Barnacle was her name—
or it might have been some other girl
waiting to cross not redhead
but raven haired we don't know
a few seconds making all seem (im)possible
for that matter a street in Dublin
on a day unlike another, June 16th,
to be exact, 1904

and the street is lost and the people in it

and Jap asks, "According to what?"

Visual Dialectic or "photographer unknown"

for Eliane Kunzi
and for Amedeo Modigliani

It is in the
rapid
acquisition
in the eyes—

everything else follows
from that,

and in a given stance,

something
beautiful
about
a woman being
attentive to the
man she's with—

the reaching over
with napkin
to wipe
the man's lips

the knees and/
or hands
touching
under table   arm around shoulder

the alert, seemingly serious conversation
as though they are almost hidden—

the meaningful account of themselves

the *coup de foudre* on their faces.

The time is 4:17

There is this isolated photo—

probably taken impromptu
   by street photographer—

as they were coming out of
the restaurant

but exactly *when*
cannot be determined

the negative is lost.
The print is of poor quality, pockmarked with grain.

The expressions of the faces barely readable,
so you can't make out the emotion
or perhaps what's said
         as they wait
                  to cross the street—

                  the cool breeze
                     hitting the sides of the heads
                        before rain comes

will they separate
or go back to his rooms

will she stay the night
  or make excuse for
     leaving
        before daybreak, etc.

were they happy or lonely?

will she deny fate,

thus negating what wld come after,

or how it wld not be
                    ten years after—having had her way

Could it have been Paris 1919?   (It feels like Paris

and being each other's only eyewitness
memory is inadequate, in this instance

or the compulsion to
turn experience itself
    into a way of seeing
                    is what
                        survives
                    as archival
                            evidence.

                                The few extant
                                    photos of her
                                        attributed to him, e.g.,

the one 8½ x 11 semi-gloss
printed full-neg,
                    set on self-timer,

shoulder touching shoulder, full-face,

they look out
at those
who unknowingly chose
to be looked at
by looking
at them

                                It is happening
                                    all over again.

Boerum Hill and Milano / Two Sightings

for Jedi

What do they have in common?
That within distinct borders someone I loved
And someone I could easily love is sleeping.
That this poem can only invent what already exists
But lacking anything further
Becomes imagined again, becomes myth
And the idea of forgetfulness reverses itself.
To start with: the sweatshirt is turned
Inside out, the outside touching the skin.
A translucent, inner glow.
The hair blond and cropped short, so the
Back of the neck is fully exposed.
Seen at a distance, the Old Egremont Club, west
On Rte.23: lives in Boerum Hill, tests
Patients HIV for a living—
Easily cld've been a fashion model. But no name.
Never got it. Never spoke a word to each other.
It's like Dante without Beatrice to be specific—
Not the unrequited sequence of events
Or the half-light of thirteenth century Italy,
But never knew she was being written about,
Watched from a small distance
On the Ponte Vecchio and then disappeared,
Like the girl with no name, like
The way someone you see once at a distance
Never leaves the mind's eye.
How long before someone discovers you're who
I'm writing about?
We reshuffle the tearsheets endlessly,
Hoping the face might somehow change.
Now the past arrives and departs on the afternoon train
Out of Rome's Ottavia station. Then it was 1968.
I remember the way she looked,

Momently, halting in step,
As if in slow-motion freeze frame
The middle of Piazza del Popolo,
The wide expanse of cobblestone reflecting bits of the sky.
She was hurrying to go somewhere.
There was so little to say and so nothing was said.
Amazing I've not given thought to Benedetta
Barzini all these years. Now suddenly
She's a person once again, like someone in 1991.
Suddenly Feltrinelli, her step-brother,
Calls out to me and I set back the clock
And he waits for me to come back.
The past is diminished.
Milano enveloped in the grey mists of an Ugo Mulas snapshot.
Milano a stone-gray of scaffolding, overhead wires,
Crowds of black umbrellas going every which way
In a futurist sunrise. Everything passes and fast.
Soon I'll forget what part Boerum Hill plays in all this.
Myth brings us back to where it all started,
Though irretrievable.
Memories someone else might read about,
Memories refusing to acknowledge personification.
History is like that.
Beatrice had no name.
You with *no-name*.
That's what we'll call you.
That's what I'm gonna have to call you.
Everything else is waiting to be invented …
Stories of passion,
Picture postcard vacations,
Prêt-à-porter soaked through from an afternoon shower
In the via Canova, a day
Unlike another, but soon soon forgotten.
The mind drifting off into the mind's eye
Surrounded by what could be,
All my time occupied,
Without the faintest idea how to find you.
Because you exist as a face only.
No matter.

Reality is unreasonable sometimes.
No one needs to remember our unnamed lives—
A series of afterimages and
The evergreens undulate as the breeze
Is happening all the while, feeds into the landscape.
This morning's gold mist is compared with nothingness.
Last year the landscape was compared with nothingness.
Last year was still one year less …
But not now. Not now as the white tanktop strap
Slips from the white shoulder, disappears
In the b&w photo, becoming an afterthought,
Slightly underexposed.
Our time come and gone I suppose—
All that we know for sure happened as not happening.
The past gives away nothing. You have to research it.
Scent of travel, flesh of experience.
Something infinite is made finite again,
A matter of setting the f-stop, adjusting the focus,
The face vertically framed for the eternal last shot.
The longer you look at the face, it reveals nothing.
It's a matter of how much of what we are
As history do we mean to believe
And how much is fantasy
The way what used to be isn't.
Empty flashbacks. Rooms filled with silence.
Last glint of sunlight in the hallway upstairs.
Somewhere in all this I know is my life:
The quiet, the sad Housatonic
Not more than 200 yards from where I now sit.
To my left Water Street Cemetery
With its tumbling granite obelisks, unfamiliar names
Like Keefe, Bracken, Giddings and Cosgrove,
Shadowed by tree limbs, a network of wires.
The past keeps erasing itself
And we all become no-names in a sense.
The neighbor's mower thrums till its almost music
Is that of a silence—roof silhouettes, a dog barking,
Traffic from Rte. 7 beginning to thin.
Streetlights come on early

In Barrington against an indefinite twilight.
My favorite backroad is half-hidden, cluttered
With last year's leaves, this year's broken glass.
It's April again, and 1991 again,
Boerum Hill and Milano
And the Berkshires also come to think of it.
I can still imagine what it's like reliving the future
And now the sun comes out and I'm back in my chair.
See now ... I've almost forgotten her name,
The girl with no-name.

Ben Maddow Speaks

for Tina Modotti

Her life turns up in many accounts
of Mexican life in the twenties.
She is a woman of great physical beauty
and personal dynamism.
Her best-known picture is the "Staircase"
taken in Mexico in the twenties.
She was a dedicated Communist—
in Mexico and in Moscow
and in Spain during the Civil War.

Born in northern Italy in 1896,
emigrated to San Francisco at age 17.
Four years later she married Ronbaix
(Robo) de l'Brie Richey.
They moved to Los Angeles.
She worked briefly as a starlet
in a number
of Hollywood movies.
She met Edward Weston.
She became his lover.
He encouraged her to take up photography.
He instructed her and was responsible
for the standards she observed.
She died in 1942 allegedly of a heart attack
in a taxi late one night,
in Mexico City,
although foul play was suspected
but could never be proved.

Dans les espaces de marées d'un corps qui se dévêt.
—Paul Eluard
(from Man Ray*)*

The Invisible Photographs

What many cannot forget are her eyes.
She stands, feet planted firmly, the body
profiled on the far left of a grainy black & white photo.
Or she's standing wide-eyed behind a steamy pane of blue glass.
One hand touching the window through clouds.
The nape of a neck that rises steeply,
the tender curve of the skin behind the ear.
The hair close-cropped.
These are your attributes. These are your mysteries.
That's how Dick Avedon described you.
He said the mirror looks at you,
so the mirror looks at you.
You collect yourself.
Carefully, as if buttoning a shirt—the last button,
you compose your features.
It's a whole communion of perfumes and phrases,
of thoughts and of breathing. The eyes now averted.
The exposure double-checked: 60th at f/5.6 or eleven.
The film-speed is grainy and fast.
Rumpled tanktop.
The mauve light washing the walls.
I have never, to my mind, known anyone named Alexis Barth.

Poem in Italian

Donna Giada Ruspoli,

youngest beauty of a princely Roman family... tall,

slender, seventeen; daughter of Don Sforza and Donna

Domitilla Ruspoli. She has flowing dark-gold hair, violet-

blue eyes, side-set in a fantastic sweep of lashes. In her

face now are the reserve and mystery of youth; in her body,

its quick grace and energy... For this photograph

by Avedon, Donna Giada wore makeup

for the fourth time in her life.

Endangered Species

This is not a picture of Kay Boyle and
                    Harry Crosby
            at Le Moulin de Soleil
    Ermenonville, France, Winter 1929.
That one can be found in the
Special Collections / Morris Library
Southern Illinois University, Carbondale.
This one was made in the photomaton,
6ᵉ Arrondissement, near Cafe Flore.
Perhaps it's the way they don't look at each other
makes everyone believe that there's
real incompatibility between them.
Misappropriated, mislabeled
until eighty years later,
it's the only proof that they were together.

Some Things to Remember about Tri-X

for Virginia Vincent

... but not everything is that predictable:

The wet heat of an armpit, for instance

handsome breasts rising

fingers that touch

slope of back, shoulders

caressing the feet, the hands

the smell of all that goes
        into memory of self

hand resting on thigh

ankles crossed, naked eyes

Sound of wind through tops of trees
        in Reineke's yard

and there were birds this morning
early and a bit of rain too

the secret parfum

the questions are not wrong

And there are magical differences too.
She smokes. I don't. Cigarettes, that is

And someone holds her face up

for a kiss

and days later someone
can't quite get to sleep—*wonder who that is?*

Finally the stars
flicker and go out.

A dream is waking

      So
it's not very strange
that the photo is always there
when one looks out the window, it
being morning

and to see the clouds and mountains
in the motionless distance...

                    I am back at my "spot"

not the Weesperzijde. 2 Anderson Street.

Time is racing.

What time is it now?

The cats move quietly about the house.

A wind comes in from the north
      but softly.

The mountains fade into light.

Old hawk-eye circles above

I rise early

coffee, my first cup of the day,

stare out at East Mountain

Try not to think. Laugh inside.

What do all these things
    have to do with photography?

What do all these things have
    in common?

18 February 1994

not the 19th is André Breton's birthday

acknowledged founder of Surrealism

which would have made him 98 today

but that's not the real reason

for writing this poem

There's this snapshot see a moment when it's completely dark
When a cloudbank passes in front of the sun
So André his wife Elisa their heads back-lit
In open shade the white oak singing the heated begonias
It appears they have just finished lunch
On a hillock sloping out back
A friend's cottage in Neuilly-sur-Seine
They have their differences but they have a life
Together that is to say they're wearing each other's pyjamas
Here he continually turns back on his childhood
A primary source for the dream
And she

When she bends down
I can see her breasts caressed by shadows of light
Through the folds of the blouse
Her beauty spills over
Warm and perfumed areolae bronze-like in color
The day is beautiful
Broad-shouldered tendrils of hair
Free-flowing over her face
Blaise Cendrars once remarked
Elisa has the most beautiful breasts in the world
"Le lot corse," is how he put it

Others characterize her as légère trompeuse
Factice sans sincérité

She has no fear
Of loving or of taking
She also knows how to give
Often I imagine what it might've been like
He had written a poem, "My Wife"
It's supposed to've appeared
An edition of three dedicated to Marcel
Duchamp whose favorite number *is* 3
But none survive and the manuscript has never been found

I study the photograph for a long time
Elisa appears to be dark and quiet and serious
Her eyes even look down perhaps avoiding glare
Of the two o'clock sun this picture bears
A striking resemblance to others
In the history of photogenic romance

So there's this deep solitude in her face
I noted passing her once in the rue des Archives (3ᵉ)
Elisa speaks to no one I'm told
She won't even come to the phone what gives
She came from a broken home brother mother no one else
She remembers nothing else
Was she a nice person is pure speculation
She's less a character than continual temptation
But the game is up she never played fair

She roamed the quais at night
And photographed street gangs preying on tourists
She'd bum a cigarette now and then even after
She quit smoking her teeth had gone yellow

It's alleged Elisa once asked of her husband,

       "Who will replace us?"

André's answer: "Who knows, maybe no one."

XII. from Bosnia and Herzegovina
(unpublished)

2000

1990

1980

1970

1960

The Life and Death of a Photograph

In the black and white photo by Darko Bandić,
a stringer for the Associated Press,
a Muslim girl who appeared to be about 20
made her way into a grove of trees during the night
and hanged herself out of desperation.
Her body was taken to the police station
in Tuzla, where it remained
unclaimed, unidentified.

She did not see the morning light.

Suddenly she realized she was losing her life,
but that was her choice,
maimed with a fear of not knowing what next. The voice
suddenly drops off ...
                    Is it the only way out?

There is no wind in the trees.
There are no cast shadows.
The sun is directly overhead.

"If only I could hide when I jump in the void,"

and at this point she must have been almost fearless,
and then she did jump, or rather
how she managed to boost herself up
off the ground
                    for the rope to catch ...

the optic nerve fades.

At this instant, no one remembers.

No one was looking.
No one was paying any real attention.
No one said, "Don't go."

Had she stopped for a second,
up ahead was a pond
and that might have been enough to distract her,
quench her thirst, cool her face
and shoulders, cause her to forget
the reason she sought this place
before making that one clumsy leap into dark inner space.
It was night …

                    and then it was morning
… and instead, turn back,
walk down the hillock,
rejoin her friends, laugh a little maybe,
board the bus, look out the window
at the clearing sky, take a nap.
Forget that she even thought to look back.

The bus disappears
where once wagons rumbled,
where once neighbor greeted neighbor.
A road of sharp pebbles and stones.

They say nobody died and this never happens.

I have never seen your face.
I have never seen you shopping.
I have never seen you laughing with friends.
I have never seen such a clear day as this.
I have never felt the rain on my face
the way you feel the rain on your face.
I have never seen such mountains as these.
The morning heavy with dew.
I have never dreamt the dreams that you dream.

You seemed in a hurry to want to die
without realizing
the consequence, as if
already dead inside
you felt nothing further.

Suddenly all is quiet again,
except for the birds,
a cool breeze
off the Adriatic.
It's what happens
when the trees soundlessly flutter,
when the wind ravels your hair.
Another day will stand for today
that you will not witness.
There's no apartment to go back to.
No open yard. No open arms.
No shopping to be done.
No laundry, no time for mint tea
at nearby cafe.
No country walks.
No last-minute thoughts.
No more differences to be put aside.
No regrets even.

No picnics, no sweetheart.

No daydreams.

You will not know the day after today.
You will not know any more than you do now,
yet the emptiness will always be with you.

Only after death eludes us
does the photo of you make sense.
Not the bare feet on the grass.
Not the shopkeeper's dress, the kitchen dress, the holiday dress.

Not so that you'd notice
what was camouflaged against what—
was it the way you appeared to be standing
or floating in air,
facing the tree,
though one with the tree,
face-frozen, suspended in air?

Life is wholesale.
Life is cheap.

The afternoon holds no regrets.
The afternoon holds no flashbacks.
It's not enough, finally, to turn
and walk back to the crowd of terrified
women and children,
mob militias are doing their scum,
performing their lies,
returning home to their wives
and children as if
not much happened this day,
with bloodshot eyes,
muddy, wet, unshaven,
standing momentarily at the woodpile,
flicking a cigarette ash, taking a piss
out back. Their eyes
hold no flashbacks.
The wells and mine-shafts hold no screams.
The landscape holds no sounds
much like the one I find you in
now.

And there you were.
For all we know it could have been
the early nineteenth century,
though the shoes are a dead giveaway,
or the fact that your photograph places you
ahead of the lie
photos can easily disguise.

Just the stirring of the shadow
under you was cause for hope,
though I was hopelessly mistaken.

To photograph you
requires a bit of grace,
a bit of luck,

and in the course of it
I've nearly run out of film,
so the one shot lasts and lasts.
You seemed to be in a hurry
as I am now,
yet you stopped and everything
around you did too.
The birds stopped making a ruckus
and the wind off the Adriatic
and too many trees were involved,
though which one … they all look alike,
they all dance alike.

It's rare such a picture exists this way.
This was the past.
Now all is silence.
We are rushed from an open space to tall grass,
but what does this tell us?
There are things I still haven't asked.
What is the sequel?
What speed film shall I use?

So what went wrong?
So I feel disconnected.

Take me out of this forest where no one can find you.
Take me back to the dream of you living.

True, it is only a picture,
but you were there to be photographed.
You had a life.
You rejoiced with your little cousins, your neighbors.
You planted seeds in your garden,
You prepared all the meals, set the table. You prayed,
read books. You even dreamed a little.
You didn't dream for this day.
You didn't dream it would come to this.
You didn't ask for this.

There has to be no end to the story.
I owe you that,
stranger that I am,
human that I am.

November 21, 1995

The War is over, there is a clear victor
and those charged are in custody.

It is a bitter cold, grey autumn weekend.
Leaves blanket the ground.

In the distance, a group of kids
play cops and robbers,
chasing each other around.

Across the small park,
in a makeshift courtroom
the headphones to hear
translation of the proceedings
remain on the long wooden desk.

Some pieces of note-paper, a few pencils, one clipboard.

For the moment the dock remains empty.

This is not The Hague in 1995,
but Nuremberg, Germany, fifty years ago today.

Mladić and Karadžić and Milosević are not *in the dock*.

They are not wearing headphones
to hear the Serbo-Croatian translation
of the proceedings.

It's Sunday and they are wearing their Sunday best,
enjoying family and friends.

They are not in custody.

"The banality of evil" is still fully in charge.

What has no conscience is the refusal to remember
and time erases memory.

The dock is empty.

The black & white photo is empty.

Videotape has an archival life of 5 years.

Bosnia has always been a war of deception.

Who are the cops and who are the robbers?

How quietly everything is denied.

How artfully everything gets reinvented.

XIII.
Memory's
Snapshots,
1990–2000

2000

1990

1980

1970

1960

Robert (Mapplethorpe), remember when

      ... the eyes of them both were
opened, and they knew that they were
naked; and they sewed fig leaves to-
gether, and made themselves aprons.
      8 And they heard the voice of the Al-
mighty walking in the garden in the
cool of the day; and Adam and his wife
hid themselves from the presence of
the Almighty among the trees of the
garden.
      9 And the Almighty called to
Adam and said to him, Where art
thou?
      10 And he said, I heard your voice in
the garden, and I was afraid, because I
was naked; I hid myself.
      11 And he said, Who told you that
you are naked?

A: The puritans of America,
     persecutors driven
     from Holland
in 1621,
         to deny

         the depth

         of what

         America
         would
         become,

     The deeper story—
flesh suppressed into shadow,
            so that today on the Green River

Robert would have delighted in knowing
he was topic of conversation,
Great Barrington township, est. 1761
—photography not yet invented—
'cept as previsualizing the nude
wading knee-deep in mind's eye idyllic—
                        a woman
in her sixties, grandmother
no doubt, stretched out on terry
cloth in unconscious atti-
tudinal pose, commenting *How if enough*
              people were to picket the pictures
in question Boston's I.C.A.,
there wouldn't be all this attention
Bright, huh?

All children are beautiful in the eyes of God
but I'm not God, surely you're not, Robert—
Likewise Lewis Carroll
capturing adolescence before threatened
by young adulthood,
                        previously invisible to the human eye

until a method by wch all was made known: the distance
separating Eakins from his holiday
swimmers, recalling memories and
associations dreamlike, the Green River
                        then and now,
                        or the privileged intimacy
of Balthus:
              child's play
          or the play of light and
          deep shadow
              on human
                  flesh, the beads of
              water on shoulder/
                      collarbone
                      catching
                      the light,

                    vagina catching the
light "fixed for ever
in the position, destined
for a single instant to occupy,"*
the labial folds like the closed wings of a butterfly
not fully developed—
                    tuckt under
pubic arch
                    whose anatomical structure
remarked Freud: "Anatomy is destiny"
thoroughbreds of a type, families by the sea
found at Cap d'Agde, the south of France.

Suddenly the viewer brought close w/the children
depicted. No harm done. Ever.
See the smile in their eyes.

        Must we be forever condemned
for exploring the ephemeral
in a girl of ten
ten years hence
swimsuit accentuating
the hints of cuts
her body will become?

"But then," thought Alice,
"shall I *never* get any older
than I am now?"

---

*William Henry Fox Talbot, 1839.

Morning of January 2, 1993

Why would Danny Campana speak to me
through early morning dream forty years later
as intimate friend?
His words heard not as words,
but as needing help.

He would have to be nearly my mom's age now—87.
Maybe a bit older even ... I don't know.
It was to have been my last summer
vacation in the Catskills I recall,

and now being delivery boy
for Danny's Fruit & Vegetable Produce—
slope of East 194th Street, the Bronx—
would last well into the 7th grade,
Creston Junior High.

To me I was just a kid in his eyes,
simply in his employ, like they say,
defined by a chance at proving myself
and earning my way for the first time.
I could ride a bike. Beyond that,
nothing defined us as close.

Rugged, good looks, charming, sweep of black hair
turning gray at the edges—a lit cigarette, a CAMEL,
dangling from his lips whenever I'd see him
lift bushels of produce
in or out of the store,
ring up the register,
take a breather, now and then, out back
where I'd hang out too,
between orders.

My mom was a regular customer.
They got on well.

She had good credit.

Where is Danny Campana
who touched me this morning with his soul ...

whose spirit visits me now?

Where is he now?

What is the message he brings
for me to decipher?

Why me?

What is he to be remembered for?

What is this thing called dream?

This Never Happens

     Had Mallarmé passed a demoiselle
on a back road Neuilly-sur-Seine
when he wrote
A THROW OF THE DICE
NEVER
WILL ABOLISH
CHANCE or words to that effect,
show windows reflective what's behind us
in the long, gray afternoon light

Railroad Street becoming Paris
outdoor cafe for an instant

Maia, Alexis

Beatrice Portinari diagonally crossing the street   [who else invoke?

the scent of armpit and hair

Nothing of the event
might've been
completed,
taken place

had we looked elsewhere
at exactly that moment,

or had Mallarmé
not gone out for his afternoon walk:

Would you agree?

We're talking the latter half
of the 19th century, say
around 1888,

future accounts
lost in time

or time elapsed.

THIS NEVER HAPPENS.

WHAT NEVER HAPPENS?

This Is for Asako's Notebook

It started with Ira's remark,
telling Asako that this could be the very last frame
in the photo of her
                    in his camera,
or it's another day entirely: a near
fatal accident on Rte 23
would have extended the mythologies
beyond how we see
ourselves that one instant,

and then we come out of it all,
like a sun hidden behind cloud
                              suddenly reappears.
This is a rite of passage.
This is the news photo of a young Muslim girl

facing a tree

with feet barely touching the ground:

a shadow that would account for the space
between life and death.

I never stop pointing
out photos to you.

This is for Asako's notebook.
This is for every photograph you will ever see.

This is for the resurrection and the life.

This is for the golden hour.

This is for the many fields of corn
grown higher

for the sudden rain,

the Berkshires backroads

the Green River

the Country Store.

This is for one parking ticket.

This is for the face in the mirror.

This is for stepping backwards into the mirror.

William Burroughs, 1914–1997

The day Eban jumped up
into your lap is drifting away

or whenever we meet you'd ask. "How's Eban?"

All the catbooks are drifting away:—

Chartreux, black alley cats, Burmese, Ethiopian

The Cat Inside

The cat book I was saving to give you   is drifting away
Your passion is drifting away
All the photographs are drifting away.

The road beyond is slipping away.

I saw Godard's *Le Mépris* on the day Bill died.

Bill placed his recorder right next to mine—
says "With just one there's the chance
it'll get lost, proving this conversation
never took place ..."

so this is half a poem
not existing. So this is Bill speaking,
so this is not quite finished,
                    not quite begun.

"All past is fiction."

The cut-ups are drifting away.

Today, humid, in the upper nineties

Long Island Sound
a bit milder inland
humidity at 77
94 degrees Fahrenheit

clouds, waves choppy

Greed

If markets come into being
for the things that people want,
then "affordable housing" has always been
an inalienable right.

New York City landlords
have exploited the need
by marginalizing the needy
while their coffers overflow.

State Senator Joseph Bruno,
a mark in their pocket,
could be named for a dog,
but you'd never know it. Bow-wow-wow.

"Social engineering"
would utter from his lips
in the Albany Chamber,
in the governor's office.

Evenings he'd look out
over his one-hundred-plus acre estate
in Rensselaer County,
one-hundred-forty miles from New York.
Not a human in sight, not a cloud in the sky.

From the Drancy transit camp near Paris
the last freight train departs for points
unknown to its human cargo.
The year is 1944.
Social engineering: *lebensraum* for the well-to-do.

L'Histoire de Paris

Why suddenly ...?
Haussmann had nothing to do with it.
In any event the avenues would have continued
and later, anyone attempting a barricade
would have been in for a big surprise.
The cars and the dust would eventually change all that.
How quickly the years pass.
How quickly the rue du Faubourg-Saint-Honoré
ascends into the outskirts, yet the tram tracks
remain, some puddles reflecting an infinite sky—
a bit darker perhaps than if we looked up,
as though the whole surface were haunted
by someone stepping out of a taxi and splash.
It's all there, like little pieces of newspaper
and yesterday's trash to be collected
and the gutters hosed down.
For it seems that all moments are like this:
the dreaminess of rain-reflected lights
gives way to a change of light, a rosy dawn,
or the few photographs someone else leaves behind
for someone else to reflect.
We haven't a clue as to who you are,
or on which corner or under which streetlamp.
Then, it doesn't matter that the photos come
in the wrong order: the sound of the typewriter
keys dissolving into the faint rumbling of the Metro,
the muffling of all noise in the heat of the morning.
About that day ... but all this comes as no surprise.

Café Gitane

for Nini?

We stare across oceans and time zones,
date-lines, pages of poetry.
We stare across each other's field of vision
We stare across the choppy silence
across double-takes, mistaken identities, tradition.
We stare across the unexplainable and the unforeseeable.
We stare across the body language
and we know right away or we don't. The repose.
The tilt and turn of the head, in your mom's likeness.
The hair jet-black, in a chignon.
Small-breasted, slender, under black cashmere.
We stare through the eyes of strangers.
A face not entirely yours. An aura undeniably yours.
Eyes lowered. We stare
across b&w photostrips, through park fences,
through windows, through backlit window reflections,
through the waking hour, the golden hour,
beyond rumpled sheets, beyond the twist of fate.
Through cat eyes and almond eyes
through photographs.

We stare across the dream till it exists.

We stare across the Seine,
across dark rooftops, the thunder and flash,
across fast-moving clouds.

In a matter of minutes we stare at nothing,
thinking of nothing. We look away.

I am back in my chair.

I get up to leave. A quick last glance.

No more staring. No more imagining.

For all I know I've mistaken you
for someone I have never seen.

The 3rd Avenue El

for Frank Kuenstler, 1928–1996

First, it was the street's surface in perpetual twilight.

Everything was in high contrast,
the trestle and cross-ties,
the wood planking.

I can't remember the faces now, none of them.
Can't remember what was said,
what was read in the papers.

Can't remember the rattan seats, the bare lightbulbs,

the station interiors with potbelly stoves.

Can't remember the straphangers,
the bodies all bundled up, the overhead fans,
the darkening sky.

The erratic rumbling of the wood C-types,
a three to six car express
                            having just cleared the switch.

The past cancelled out because no one remembers,

so the past is imagined.

Light dispelling the gloom.

Buildings flee backwards, tracks & switches,
signals, reflected windows,
the view out the window,

vestigial remains of abandoned approaches

at Chatham Square junction.

Always a child's question. What comes next?

Why are some shades drawn and not others?

Who is that woman leaning out on her elbows?

Will I see her again
next time? When is next time? What comes next?

No one thought to look for me
wrapped in my imagination with my face pressed to the glass
at the very front of the train.

The rails awash with rain.

And no one remembers.

The last sounds
of the El, and then an eternity of silence.

What made me think to take these pictures now anyway?

Even hold a camera at twelve?

And why would I want to?

Was it a matter of luck, chance, then?

So we print the same negative over and over
till it yields something else.

Imagined futures. Imagined past. The aura of loss.

Always strangers facing each other in the light and dark.

Always the light of the late afternoon slicing through girders.

All that I remember seeing in photographs,

all of the above.

What we collect
is the measure of what we forget.

With Frank dead, who will I relate this to?

So I'm making believe these photos never happened—
that I never pressed the shutter release
to let the light in,
to let the reality I see that one instant
become that one instant
at the long end of day, at the rush-hour.

The following year I turned 13
didn't think of the El much.

It's another era,

almost another century.

Italian Superstitious

This should've been your poem, not my poem.
Should've been the Highland movie
marquee draped in blue and red neon—
Not some fucking hole in the ground.
This should have been the life of Joseph Anella,
not the crow crashed through his back bedroom window—
not the dizzy free-fall to the ground. The bird stunned.
The wings napping.
Not my dad giving the ritual birdbath
to finally set the bird soaring.
This should have been the Life of Joe, not a black omen.
Should've been the New York, New Haven & Hartford
spanning the Hudson,
not some rusted skeleton—
splinters of light pouring through the transverse at noon,
through the silence.

I don't know Joe Anella.
He was 23.
He died in his sleep.

Molly Goldberg Once Lived Here

It wasn't clear in which room the photos were stored,
or did the apartment exist at all.

The street you barely saw from three stories above,
and in the blink of an eye it's all gone, leaving behind
a feeling that something existed here once, like the wind
tearing through clotheslines, like the rumble from somewhere above.

One can only imagine the trusses,
supports creating a crosshatch of lights
and darks, striating the morning gloom;
the same sunlight slicing through
dust-bleached windows overlooking the El tracks.

So history constantly shifts
and then we don't know where we are anymore.
And still the district extends, deeper and deeper
into the dream of everyday life.
The smash of domino, a car backfires, childish pranks,
the clipclopping of horses on cobblestone,
all candy and cigarettes, ticket stubs,
the make-believe ballroom on Webster Ave.

But I'm ahead of myself.
I'd have to go back to see such-and-such street still exists,
if someone kept records, if in going a little too far
in one direction, I'd find my way back to Rose Hill Park.

Memory transformed into fireflies
and faces remain recognizable for that one instant
before the lights turn out and the neon takes over,
casting its glow on the sidewalk.

A door opens far down in the hall
and a very old lady appears in a faded housedress
and one wakes up and everything seems ordinary again.

Girl with a Box Camera

"What have you got there in your hand?"

"It's a camera."

There is the eleven-year-old girl playing hopscotch or jacks
on the sidewalk.
There is the billboard torn to shreds
and pieces of darkness.
There is blinking neon.

All the pictures to be taken,
the darkness hugging the edges; the millions of faces.

There are cuts and more cuts. There are retakes.

What's meant is that the past
returns the full image of who you are with nothing left over
and this existence absorbs you
and then the sunlight ends and begins again.

So the photograph is never without what the moment would be—
a kind of rehearsal for how the past comes into focus.
Perhaps some cloud-cover.
Perhaps the street caught in the slanting angle of light.

Life, as it recedes, becomes shorter.
The traffic jam, for one thing, seems to allow for second thoughts
about an awakening of sorts.
These cloud shapes filling up an avalanche of tears and debris,

and now they too collapse into nonbeing,
rushing past, backlit against a silver-gray sky.

Is there no memory for this?

Does the moment have an existence
separate from what it reflects?

A silhouette of a man crosses the street
under the El bathed in a dusty, yellow light.
He is on his way and you have just taken his picture
and the light has already gone from there too.

The Arcades Project, unfinished

"Honey, where are you going?"

"Out for a walk."

I am a camera
recording, not thinking.

     In Paris I had the distinct feeling we'd met before.
I was crossing blvd St.-Germain
when suddenly seeing you there
I'd also recognized Monsieur Verne at the far
     edge of the sidewalk
looking up at the sky,
though you didn't see him
and seeing as you caught my eye
first, we'd find our way to the Flore.

A bicyclist completes this sequence before
we're able to sit down.
At first, we observe the crowd
and the waiter takes our order—one le russe, one cognac.
I'd just completed my investigation
into a crime unsolved for some years.
What better way to celebrate than to sit with you now.

Good thing we did.
We didn't expect the stormfront to move in so quickly.
We didn't expect to have our picture taken,
because photography was still young—
because I often walk alone through the streets
and take note of the storefronts,
the hundreds of faces, the well-to-do,

and this was Paris, not Berlin, 1866
and overhead wires had not yet dissected the sky—
the affiche torn to shreds

revealing old news.

I am a secret witness. I am curious.
I am one whose eyes are guided by the incessant flow of traffic.
I see the whisked lights of the city.

I take pictures
I am a camera
recording.

I enter shop after shop,
price nothing
speak no word,
and look at everything with a wild and vacant stare.
I look at my watch.

Who will make sense out of this?

Who will remember me?

Where will you find me?

For a few seconds I stare at my reflection in a shop window.
For a few seconds I don't recognize myself.

No idea where my walking would take me.

Always the same stopping.
Always the same returning.

On the blvd Raspail apartment buildings
    with their tall windows reflecting the grey sky.

    I realize immediately that by setting out
I shouldn't have anything too specific
in mind,
but to simply take in my surroundings
with each turn of the corner
until people's faces, shop windows, displays,

the affiches of different sizes
and colors become one textural maze.

Did photography change the way we would remember
these sites?

The Passage Choiseul is still with us,
A day of visual impressions is still with us.

What is the scene of traffic circles?

What is the focal point that structures the angles
and aspects of life in the street?

What is the art of taking a walk?

When did public transportation, when did the street
signals come into existence
the METRO rumbling aboveground
When did we learn how to cross the street
When was the street extended
When did night—
When did the illumination of night erase what was night
When is what you see a reflection
                              of what you see
When did the first gaze occur
       and on which street

What are you left with?

Patterns of pavement, branches of trees
silhouetted, traces of rain running down fading façades.

"You're back ... and what did you see?"

"Not much. Filled out a report."

There are no neon lights and running letters.
There are no electrical tramways no electrical grids,

no overhead wires dissecting the sky,
or a person passing by, often by chance,
the various locales not yet familiar.

There are no park benches covered in a blanket of leaves
Place des Vosges
no byways and alleyways that I would remember—
no crime scene,
no slate pavements of irregular shapes.
There are no street-texts, the traces of shadows,
the silhouettes of people,
the tired glances of people rushing past.

There are no figures standing still, talking or walking.

There are no predetermined routes, or rain-reflected lights.
No red lights or blue lights.
No more aimlessness,

demolition scaffoldings, construction site fencings,
     et cetera,
and so there is less of a distance.

Who might have seen what I see now,
     not knowing the difference?

Who might remember the shop windows,
The turning of streets, the unexpected arcades?

A seemingly inconspicuous alley
a dirt-covered roadway, the flow
of rush-hour traffic, the slow
motion twilight, the METRO

… and the passing day falls.

The aura of things. The aimless reflections.

What is disappearing

What is being replaced
What is the pleasure of slowness

What is its measure?

    The storm had let up
with red at the edges. The sky was now a deep blue.
The twilight was soon coming on.
M. Baudelaire got up from his chair—
said something about *next time.*
As he walked down the street towards the rue de Rennes
he stopped momentarily
in front of a shop window,
then looked to the left and to the right
and possibly thinking the reflection was someone he knew,
tipped his hat, turned
                  and was suddenly gone

into the passing crowd, into the hazy twilight.

The Council Flats

It felt suddenly like November '95.
We were leaving on a journey by rented car, heading west.
Each memory is a grainy picture.
Shall we try just once more to retrace our steps?
The stretches of time are different
and so the landscape behaves differently.
Today fast moving clouds above the heath on the road to Portlevan.
Tomorrow, The Lizard.
What did we eat we went shopping at *Tesco*.
A blue wind was coming in off the sea.
Afterwards the sound of typewriter keys.
Now for the darkness and for the darkness in dreams.
Waves crashing low sounds of gulls.
Where are the Council Flats in all this?
Where are the tracks?

The Riddle of 16 Silver Double Elvis Paintings

In 1963 Andy and I silkscreened
eleven Elvis paintings in preparation
for the show at Ferus Gallery, L.A.

While visiting Cecil Beaton at his bungalow
in the Beverly Hills Hotel
he showed us a book of his b&w portraits,
one of which had been superimposed 3 times over, maybe more,
coincident with the portraits already made:
Triple Elvis, Elvis 1 and 2, Elvis Three Times Over.

Always, in all these paintings
Elvis's head and the tip of his boots
touched the edge of the canvas
when stretched.
                  Likewise, all were signed
on the verso.
                  Always 82 inches in height ... always.

Nearly ten years after Andy's death 1987,
from seemingly nowhere
16 *Double Elvis* paintings surface,
all identical in that
the full figure floats
in the center of a muddy silver haze.
The head and boot-tips
all ill-positioned.
                  The canvases remain
conspicuously unsigned.

Each painting is certified
by the Warhol Foundation
as authentic.

What happened to the 82 inches?

What is the riddle?

Who's gonna know the difference?

Leo Dies

Leo dies.

Not today.
Not amidst the chalk marks, stickball bats,

not unlike the silence in a zoning photograph,

the slanting rays of light, the roar
of the echoing El not four
blocks distant,
              the light that pours

through open slats.

Not the family summer house, the towers

of books, the folklore.
              The June showers.

The Adriatic not far distant
and the sinewy trees. The path overgrown.

The long bicycle-walks superimposed against a now distant sky.

The trailing grasses. The early, green apples.

From earliest childhood,

July. No, August. Not the picnic's distant laughter,
empty swings swaying,
the hide-and-seek games toward summer's end
and soon nothing remaining.
              The clover covered with frost.

Not biding one's time

in a bank, perchance to dream, imagine

through beveled glass … the remaining voices trail off.

Not the uncertainty.

Not now, not 1948.

Not man's fate.

The hundred and hundreds of flowers,

the targets and flags

not for sale. Not slow to forget.

Not to know. Not to be looking.

Not sleight-of-hand,

the plotting-and-scheming backrooms.

Not the darkness at noon.

Not … not because the alarm goes off

and everything is back where it was,

and it's later now. Not nearly a century.

No special privileges. Not the art.

Not to see it coming. Not today.

ALgonquin 4-8692

Marcel Duchamp phoned and I called him back:
ALgonquin 4-8692.
He had me come to have a look,
to pass the test, to dream.
He had this idea for constructing a kind of diorama,
more like a 3-dimensional photograph,
representing one day out-of-doors
in early autumn and preoccupied for some time
with preparatory notes that were more a puzzle
of instructions than anything having to do finally
with the way the whole piece was slowly evolving.
Into what, I wonder?
The landscape was scrupulously clean.
The leaves were mostly birch, rust-colored.
The horizon seemed out of reach, simply there was none.
Further back a warren of fir trees, frost-bitten.
Some thistle and shrub.
The keyhole was not fabricated or attached in any way, as I recall.
The waterfall part was off to one side, waiting to be installed.
It was all in the open, waist-level,
and all kinds of discarded objects cluttered the floor.
What we had before us was the body-mold of a woman
naked, a young girl really, knees akimbo in the unweeded grass.
The wave of blond hair. The face turned away.
The shaved pubis concealed and revealed simultaneously,
but in no ways a focal point.
                              So much else was going on,
like a modern-day Brueghel, it was hard to keep track.
Still, you got the sense it could only happen here.
And here she is lying on her back in the thorny twigs
with outstretched arm and hand reaching up
and holding what appears to be a gas lamp
and what I really saw—she was reaching up, yes,
but to turn down the light, as if the panorama behind her
was merely a backdrop, a baby-blue sky, which it was
and with sun coming up, a kind of idyllic landscape

coming to a close as a kind of fade-out,
anticipating that we would see her no more,
except maybe as a dream in which memory evaporates.
Still, she seemed very much alone.
What we had before us
was a landscape booby-trapped with other stories also.
I can't tell you which ones.
Each moment is the true one from how depth of field is calibrated.
There was no way to see it in its complete state
before dismantled, shipped off
until much later and it would be the last time
I'd spend time in his company,
though I didn't know that.
His smile was reassuring, as if sensing a poem
somewhere in all this and giving me the nod.
Now the past is already here
and I'm left with this void, more dust breeding.
Oh, and I forgot: Andy never showed up.

The Navyblue Overcoat

Jean Louis Kerouac
owned several navyblue overcoats,
one of wch he wore to his dad's funeral.
He lived in a loft facing out
onto Broadway,
                    though it went by
the name Central Park Ave
w/ an El running through it, with sunlight
slipping through the open slats of the tracks.
He was out somewhere when I arrived.
No tellin' when he'd return.
I had the time all mixed up,
the streets confused.
I could hear him coughing
as he came up the stairs.

Autumn Leaves

What do shadows and doorways have in common?

The photo could've been that of Arthur Rimbaud
photographing himself 1883 Harar
nos. 476
    477 the only two known to survive
grainy and slowly disintegrating.
He's wearing a white linen shirt
loosely fitted white trousers
and he's not wearing a hat.
He's standing in the shade just as you are now
in the cool of the doorway and backlit,
though it's fall.
Will we ever return?
Will the spot be the same?
Can we find the spot?
Can we repeat the photo?

The Nassau Loop Is No Longer Running

Take away memory and what've you got?
The invisible shapes, the street's confusion, the late quiet.
It turns out past where a block
of signals are crossed and divides
into two storage tracks and of these
one forms a continuous loop that leads nowhere
and is now hidden, goes unnoticed,
is useful to almost no one. The vacuumed air
is already gone from here like a ghost. The bare
lightbulbs flicker. Some power lost altogether
and the world begins to fade.
Nothing is stationary. Not the stairway
closed off, not the patches of tile fallen off. Not the lone
pigeon. It still gets cold. The map's been redrawn.
The lights of the train stood still and then vanished.

Meshes of the Afternoon

A game of Jacks hadn't as yet been decided.
The clothesline trails into a slow dissolve.

But by then we were walking over what seemed
a crumbling viaduct of insurmountable size
with sleds trailing behind.

It was late afternoon. The mongrel dog nearly bit me.

You sat, smiling, eating your ice cream.
Looking up, now and then, at the clock above.

The train, up ahead, disappears in a flurry of signals
and then the street begins to rise sharply.

You keep asking the same question, over and over
until the response becomes somebody's excuse
for a myth. The journal does not confirm this.

Eyes stare down from behind handpainted bifocals
and the streetlamp nestled in a grainy distance of fog.
The playground is empty.

Passage Choiseul

for Mimmo Rotella

The pulp gives way
another face shows through and then another
in the fuzz of dust as the calm darkens
and the roar of time is suddenly silenced.
That's how it all began.
The light came in under a clear sky of glass.
At this point a line is missing.
The pavement vanishes.
You move to another table
to block out the scale and dimensions of size.
Much of it's about to disappear before everyone's eyes
have chance to adjust. You reach for the cool lemonade.
So what remains are the shreds of history
emerging, concealed imaginings, frag
mented letters. Headlines. This keeps happening
throughout the autumn and the rainy season.
The paste dripping the eyes dripping.
The pieces of her head still intact.
The face older now.

It Happened Here

It happened here in Jamestown, Missouri, August 7th, 1930.
It says so on the picture postcard,
                                    now mottled, cracked in places.

Marylou Sims was standing in her flimsy yellow dress,
wide-eyed, sucking in her upper lip,
looking up. She stood among the wave of sun-filled faces,
all about her own age, 11, 12 maybe.
They appear to be enjoying themselves. Some of them.
There's even a feeling of emptiness among them,
but they wouldn't know that.

All I could see of her was the back of her neck,
the scent of lilac captured in her hair.
Blonde it was, cut short round the back—
A small lock fastened with a barrette.

She stood below off to the left,
careless about whether she'd seen or not …
the mouth ragged and spongy. Yeah.
The body naked from the waist down,
the trouser legs bunched at the knees
and the white cotton shirt rolled up under the armpits.
The lean belly, bisected by a line of dark hair.
It was perhaps her first glimpse at the limp testicles.
No one said, don't look. She continued to stare
and forget. There was no scream. Just a quick grunt
and then nothing,
as if all the blackbirds suddenly ceased to exist and the wind …
the wind died down.
The crowd quickly dispersed, the respectable local citizens.
Men in their dusty suits and straw hats heading back up the Main Street.
The shops open.
                    She'd gone fishin' with friends.

I can recall the lithe body in her flimsy yellow dress

and for all I know I've walked past Marylou—
an alert old lady I'm certain—
on some Jamestown road within the last few weeks.

Charles Henri Ford's Archive Vanishes

Henri Cartier-Bresson walks through a group of shouting schoolchildren
with Leica in hand and sleeves rolled up and then vanishes.
Tchelitchew stretching out in the glowing sand of a beach in winter
vanishes. Gertrude Stein vanishes.
Paul Eluard vanishes.
Parker ... Parker Tyler's reflection in a shop window vanishes.
The 3rd Avenue El vanishes in the gloom and then the gloom vanishes.
Joseph Cornell waiting for a bus on Utopia Parkway vanishes.
Paul Bowles vanishes in a back street in Tangiers
and Cecil Beaton waves goodbye through the rear window of a taxi.
An old lady in a black dress vanishes as the shadow of
a building falls upon her.

Sister Ruth vanishes in her sleep ...

and in the process another life vanishes.

Ernest Hemingway's Famous Lost Manuscripts, ca. 1922

It was as though the story were repeating itself,
only this time it wasn't the taxi.
Hadley's plan is to join Ernest in Lausanne for Christmas,
so she packs his mss., carbons & all,
into a small black valise. He could catch up
on his personal writing, she surmises,
in the lull between INS dispatches.
She books a compartment on the SCNF out of the Gare de Lyon.
In the heavy downpour the taxi
takes her straightaway to the station
and at the height of the rushhour
she finally manages with the help of a porter
to transport the luggage
and in that one brief instant
while out on the platform
when the bags are out of sight,
the valise with the mss is stolen.
Then it stops raining for a while. Steam rises.
The track supervisor is in the approach
inspecting the grading, the signals.
A winter twilight suddenly descends through the
dark wires, the clutter of pylons.
In the distance, a silhouette of a figure disappearing.

Somewhere in ancient France, a small black
valise collects dust in an attic,
tossed there many years earlier.
Its contents undisturbed mostly.
The carbons have molded a bit,
though the typewriter face, a Remington upright,
is still legible, but no name is attached … no one knows.

Lost Time

There is a passage by Walter Benjamin I cannot locate.
There is a street in Paris that this passage describes
lost in time.
There is a shop window reflecting back
what I see for the last time.
The affiches have long since disappeared from the tunnels.
Among the photographs in my head are some I have never taken.

No. 2

The young girl framed by an immense wooden doorway
with the No. 2 etched in blue white enamel
has just been photographed by Atget
and now he's on his way home in the twilight
and she's no longer remembered.
I never asked how she got there,
standing there as she did,
or if she lived at No.2 for a time
and was it drizzling,
or did he ever return to show her the photo.

Discard Box

We don't have a name to go with the face.
We don't have the exact place
suggesting anything other than

Someone's life ...

So they remain a family
unnamed. The older gentleman—he appears
to be patriarch
in 34 of the 44 snapshots surviving
and there's a blanked silence
of several pages and then in the last 4
he's not visible at all
and it could be another year even
and the faces seem a bit lonely.

Jacket tie boater   only on this day
his hand gently strokes the face of the horse
while staring directly into the camera

and he's off in another ... into the gloom

and the light is somewhere behind,

no longer sequenced,

no longer summer of echoing voices,
familiar nicknames, the sea
breeze off in the distance.

The card games and stories, the nameless
events. The colors of distance.

A present that's now fairly grainy
as the day dies away.

Only a few key place-names
handwritten in an elegant script
suggest holiday outings : Lake Wickaboag,
Cooperstown, Otsego Lake and the Tower.

Is the Tower still there?

Even after all this I've come up with nothing.

Does anyone know these people?

Does anyone know where
to find them?

Whose father he is?

Who took these pictures?

Who is the young girl, Irene,
seated in wheelchair
out on a sunlit lawn in a kind of flashback?

An atmosphere of convalescence seems to subsume her
bright smile ... and who
is the woman standing beside her, a "Miss Hughes"

dated 1917.

Leaving New York

for Asako

Never to piss again
out upper storey library window
at the snow below,
while standing on my desk,

                oh dear.

                No more
early morning rain. No more whistling freight

No more bleeding furnace to keep warm

No more weekend visits from Ira and the Jedi,
the silence of a windless day,
occasional trucksounds shifting gears
dogs barking

The pollen dusty air of August

No more running up and down the stairs
looking for the cats—"the boys"—they're napping

No more redwing blackbird; there'll be others.

No more cushioned sound of midnight snow
softened by the snow that fell before
    on shingled roof.

No evening star.

No family deer, to leaves to rake.

No more long twilight walks through dusty hills
performing letters in my head

I'll type up hours later, almost word for word.

No more Green River where I'd skinny-dip
not so skinny now, for sure.

No chimes at midnight.

No more power outage from electric storms.
The worst!
I just go to bed. What else to do?

One thing's certain—
no more loss, the women in my life, that is.

No more ladybugs.

No time for winter now.

No more past.

No more poems-in-progress.

There's no stand of spruce,
no immutable crickets, no juniper,
no East Mountain to gaze out on—
vapors and clouds

The sounds of screendoor slamming.

No brushing leaves.

No poems?

No more photographing you
against upstairs hallway wall
where sunlight comes
sliding through in a slow crawl.

There'll be other kinds of photographs,

other kinds of dreams.

No two days the same.

No more the fresh faint smell
  of coming summer rain.

No great loss.

I never really wrote about this anyway.

Printed June 2001 in Santa Barbara &
Ann Arbor for the Black Sparrow Press by
Mackintosh Typography & Edwards Brothers Inc.
Text set in Giovanni and Klang by Words Worth.
Design by Barbara Martin.
This first edition is published in paper wrappers;
there are 200 hardcover trade copies;
100 hardcover copies have been numbered & signed
by the author; & there are 26 lettered copies
handbound in boards by Earle Gray each with
an original signed and numbered photograph
by Gerard Malanga.

PHOTO: Asako

GERARD MALANGA was born in 1943 and raised in the Bronx, New York, the only child of Italian immigrant parents. He is the author of a dozen books of poetry spanning a 35-year period. Muriel Rukeyser has praised his work as "one of honor, humaneness and durability. He is one of the best poets of his generation." His work has appeared in *Poetry*, *Paris Review*, *Partisan Review* and *The New Yorker*.

Gerard Malanga worked closely with Andy Warhol during that artist's most creative period in the mid-Sixties. *The New York Times* called him "Warhol's most important associate." In 1964 through '66 they collaborated on the nearly 500 individual 3-minute "Screen Tests," which resulted in a selection for a book of the same name, published a year later.

Malanga's other works include *The Angus MacLise Checklist, Scopophilia: The Love of Looking, Up-Tight: The Velvet Underground Story* (co-authored with Victor Bockris), four books of photography and two Spoken Word CD compilations: *3 Weeks with My Dog* with the Belgian rock group 48 Cameras and *Up from the Archives*, both produced in 1999. Additional works in print from Black Sparrow are: *Three Diamonds* (1991) and *Mythologies of the Heart* (1996). Gerard Malanga lives in New York City. His website is www.gerardmalanga.com.